P9-EAO-876

S...
College Library
6401 Richards Ave.
Santa Fe, NM 87508

3/15/07
hard cone
$34.95.

MARKETING WARFARE

20TH ANNIVERSARY EDITION

Al Ries & Jack Trout

McGraw-Hill

New York • Chicago • San Francisco • Lisbon
London • Madrid • Mexico City • Milan • New Delhi
San Juan • Seoul • Singapore • Sydney • Toronto

The *McGraw·Hill* Companies

Copyright © 2006 by The McGraw-Hill Companies, Inc. All rights reserved. Printed in the United States of America. Except as permitted under the United States Copyright Act of 1976, no part of this publication may be reproduced or distributed in any form or by any means, or stored in a data base or retrieval system, without prior written permission of the publisher.

1234567890 DOC/DOC 098765

ISBN 0-07-146082-9

McGraw-Hill books are available at special quantity discounts to use as a premiums and sales promotions, or for use in corporate training programs. For more information, please write to the Director of Special Sales, Professional Publishing, McGraw-Hill, Two Penn Plaza, New York, NY 10121-2298. Or contact your local bookstore.

 This book is printed on recycled, acid-free paper containing a minimum of 50% recycled, de-inked fiber.

Library of Congress Cataloging-in-Publication Data

Ries, Al.
    Marketing warfare / Al Ries and Jack Trout.—20th anniversary ed.
        p. cm.
    Includes index.
    ISBN 0-07-146082-9 (alk. paper)
    1. Marketing.   2. Competition.   I. Trout, Jack.   II. Title.

HF5415.R544 2006
658.8—dc22
                                                            2005054322

Dedicated to
one of the greatest marketing strategists
the world has ever known:

Karl von Clausewitz.

Twenty years later
we'll add several other
pretty good marketing strategists
to the dedication:

Al Ries and Jack Trout

Preface

In hindsight, *Marketing Warfare* was first published in the dark ages of competition. A decade ago, the term "global economy" didn't exist. The vast array of technology that we take for granted was still a glimmer in the eyes of some silicon valley engineers. Global commerce was pretty much limited to the multi-national companies.

All that has changed. Today's marketplace makes the one we first wrote about look like a tea party. The wars are escalating and breaking out in every part of the globe. Everyone is after everyone's business everywhere.

All this means that the principles of *Marketing Warfare* are more important than ever. Companies must learn how to deal with their competitors. How to avoid strengths. How to exploit weakness.

Organizations must learn that it's not about do or die for your company. It's about making the other guy die for his company.

It's also about pursuing the right strategy. Whether you're a big, medium, or small sized company, *Marketing Warfare* will provide the strategic model for company survival into the 21st Century.

It's the kind of stuff you were never taught in business school.

Contents

Chapter 5. The nature of the battleground

Marketing battles are not fought in physical places like the aisles of a drugstore or a supermarket. Nor in the streets of cities like Detroit or Dallas. Marketing battles are fought inside the mind of the prospect. The mind is the battleground. A terrain that is tricky and difficult to understand.

Chapter 6. The strategic square

There is no one way to fight a marketing war. Rather there are four. And knowing which type of warfare to fight is the first and most important decision you can make. The type of warfare to fight depends on your position in a strategic square which can be constructed for any product category or industry.

Chapter 7. Principles of defensive warfare

Defensive warfare is a game for a marketing leader only. There are three key principles to follow, the most surprising of which is the strategy of attacking yourself and not the enemy.

Chapter 8. Principles of offensive warfare

Offensive warfare is a game for the No. 2 or No. 3 company in a field. The key principle is to find a weakness inherent in the leader's strength and attack at that point.

Chapter 9. Principles of flanking warfare

The most innovative form of marketing warfare is flanking. Over the years most of the biggest marketing successes have been flanking moves.

Chapter 10. Principles of guerrilla warfare

Most of the players in a marketing war should be guerrillas. Smaller companies can be highly successful as long as they don't try to emulate the giants in their field.

Chapter 11. The cola war

Pepsi-Cola is winning the cola war with archrival Coca-Cola. One major reason is that Coke has not been effectively utilizing its strategic advantages.

Chapter 12. The beer war

The beer business is in the process of consolidation, from hundreds of local breweries down to a handful of national ones. At a time when the smaller competitors should concentrate their forces, they are doing just the opposite.

Chapter 13. The burger war

McDonald's continues to dominate the burger business, but Burger King and Wendy's have made progress using some of the classic principles of marketing warfare.

Chapter 14. The computer war

Nobody plays the marketing warfare game as well as Big Blue. But even IBM can fall on its face when it tries to compete on a battleground it doesn't own.

Chapter 15. Strategy and tactics

As form should follow function, strategy should follow tactics. That is, the achievement of tactical results is the ultimate and only goal of a strategy. Strategy should be developed from the bottom up, not the top down. Only a general with deep, intimate knowledge of what happens on the battlefield itself is in a position to develop an effective strategy.

Chapter 16. The marketing general

Business today cries out for more field marshals, more people willing to take responsibility for planning and directing a total marketing program. Key attributes for future marketing generals are flexibility, mental courage, and boldness.

The strategic square.

 Defensive marketing warfare is for market leaders.

 Offensive marketing warfare is for No. 2 companies.

 Flanking marketing warfare is for smaller companies.

 Guerrilla marketing warfare is for local or regional companies.

Defensive warfare.

1. Only the market leader should consider playing defense.

2. The best defensive strategy is the courage to attack yourself.

3. Strong competitive moves should always be blocked.

Offensive warfare.

1. The main consideration is the strength of the leader's position.

2. Find a weakness in the leader's strength and attack at that point.

3. Launch the attack on as narrow a front as possible.

Flanking warfare.

1. A good flanking move must be made into an uncontested area.

2. Tactical surprise ought to be an important element of the plan.

3. The pursuit is as critical as the attack itself.

Guerrilla warfare.

1. Find a segment of the market
   small enough to defend.

2. No matter how successful you become,
   never act like the leader.

3. Be prepared to bugout at a
   moment's notice.

Prologue

Why republish a book that's 20 years old? Especially if that book is still in print. (The last time we checked, *Marketing Warfare* was No. 9,706 at Amazon.com.)

First of all, the book is still in print after 20 years. Most business books aren't. That fact alone makes *Marketing Warfare* worth a second look. Furthermore, in our consulting assignments, we find that many companies are overlooking the essential strategies that they should follow.

Marketing Warfare is a book about strategy. Many of our other books are heavily loaded with tactical advice. Too often, we hear of marketing disasters along the lines of, "You said this was a good idea in one of your books, but it didn't work."

Take the launch of a second brand, a tactic that we have frequently recommended. Many firms have tried second brands with little success. When we hear of such cases, we often say, "Wait a minute. You're a small company. You should be practicing guerrilla warfare. You shouldn't be acting like a leader and launching additional brands."

On the other hand, big companies often miss the opportunities provided by second brands. They want to keep the focus on the core brand, a strategy that is best pursued by a flanker or a guerrilla.

Then there are No. 2 companies that try to emulate the leaders on the mistaken assumption that "they must know what works." No. 2 companies should launch programs that are exactly the opposite of what works for a leader, a point that many marketing managers miss.

The first step in developing any marketing program is to ask yourself, "What type of war are we fighting?"

One of the heroes of this book is Karl von Clausewitz, whose own book, *On War*, was first published 172 years ago. The book is still in print and is still studied at the military academies of the world. (It was No. 13,294 at Amazon the last time we checked.)

We'd be pleased if *Marketing Warfare* lasted a fraction as long.

War belongs to the province of business competition, which is also a conflict of human interests and activities.   Karl von Clausewitz

Introduction:
Marketing is war

The best book on marketing was not written by a Harvard professor. Nor by an alumnus of General Motors, General Electric, or even Procter & Gamble.

We think the best book on marketing was written by a retired Prussian general, Karl von Clausewitz. Entitled *On War*, the 1832 book outlines the strategic principles behind all successful wars.

Clausewitz was the great philosopher of war. His ideas and concepts have lasted more than 150 years. Today, *On War* is widely quoted at places like West Point, Sandhurst, and St. Cyr.

War has changed dramatically since *On War* was first published. The tank, the airplane, the machine gun, and a host of new weapons have been introduced. Yet the ideas of Clausewitz are still as relevant today as they were in the nineteenth century.

Weapons may change, but warfare itself, as Clausewitz was first to recognize, is based on two immutable charac-

There is not a single idea in *On War* that doesn't have direct relevance in the marketing arena. As Clausewitz said, "War belongs to the province of business competition."

teristics: strategy and tactics. His clear exposition of the strategic principles of war are likely to guide military commanders well into the twenty-first century.

Marketing needs a new philosophy

The classic definition of marketing leads one to believe that marketing has to do with satisfying consumer needs and wants.

Marketing is "human activity directed at satisfying needs and wants through exchange processes," says Philip Kotler of Northwestern University.

Marketing is "the performance of business activities that direct the flow of goods and services from producer to consumer," says the American Marketing Association.

Marketing is "the performance of those activities which seek to accomplish an organization's objectives by anticipating customer or client needs and directing a flow of need-satisfying goods and services from producer to customer or client," says E. Jerome McCarthy of Michigan State University.

Perhaps the most complete explanation of the "needs and wants" theory is the definition provided by John A. Howard of Columbia University in 1973. Marketing, says Mr. Howard, is the process of: "(1) identifying customer needs, (2) conceptualizing those needs in terms of an organization's capacity to produce, (3) communicating that conceptualization to the appropriate laws of power in the organization, (4) conceptualizing the consequent output in terms of the customer needs earlier identified,

The American Marketing Association has a new definition of marketing, released in 2005: "Marketing is an organizational function and a set of processes for creating, communicating, and delivering value to customers and for managing customer relationships in ways that benefit the organization and its stakeholders." (There's still no mention of competition.)

and (5) communicating that conceptualization to the customer."

Are those the five steps on the road to marketing success today? Would identifying, conceptualizing, and communicating help American Motors compete successfully with General Motors, Ford, and Chrysler? Let alone Toyota, Datsun, Honda, and the rest of the imports?

Let's say American Motors develops a product strategy based on identifying customer needs. The result would be a line of products identical to those of General Motors, which spends millions of dollars researching the same marketplace to identify those same customer needs.

Is this what marketing is all about? The victory belongs to the side that does a better job of marketing research?

Clearly something is wrong. When American Motors ignores customer needs, the company is much more successful. The Jeep, a product borrowed from the military, is a winner. American Motors passenger cars are losers.

No focus group is likely to have conjured up the Jeep. Nor is identifying customer needs likely to help an also-ran compete with a leader.

General Motors also borrowed an idea from the military by introducing a consumer version of the Hummer, one of the few recent GM successes. Because of high gasoline prices, however, the Hummer may be a short-term success.

Becoming customer-oriented

Marketing people traditionally have been customer-oriented. Over and over again they have warned management to be customer- rather than production-oriented.

Ever since World War II, King Customer has reigned supreme in the world of marketing.

In the 1920s, business was production-oriented.

In the 1950s, business became customer-oriented.

But it's beginning to look like King Customer is dead. And like marketing people have been selling a corpse to top management.

Companies who have dutifully followed the directions of their marketing experts have seen millions of dollars disappear in valiant but disastrous customer-oriented efforts.

To see how we got into this predicament, you have to go back to the twenties when business was production-oriented. This was the heyday of Henry "You Can Have Any Color You Want As Long As It's Black" Ford.

In the production era, business discovered advertising. "Mass advertising creates mass demand which makes mass production possible," said the advertising experts.

In the aftermath of World War II, the leading companies became customer-oriented. The marketing expert was in charge and the prime minister was marketing research.

But today every company is customer-oriented. Knowing what the customer wants isn't too helpful if a dozen other companies are already serving the same customer's wants. American Motors's problem is not the customer. American Motors's problem is General Motors, Ford, Chrysler, and the imports.

Becoming competitor-oriented

To be successful today, a company must become competitor-oriented. It must look for weak points in the positions of its competitors and then launch marketing attacks against those weak points. Many recent marketing success stories illustrate this.

For example, while others were losing millions in the computer business, Digital Equipment Corporation was making millions by exploiting IBM's weakness in small computers.

Similarly, Savin established a successful beachhead in small, inexpensive copiers, a weak point in the Xerox lineup.

Today, business must become competitor-oriented. This is more evident now than it was when this book was first published 20 years ago. A good-enough product is not good enough for success. In today's marketplace, you need a competitive edge, and marketing can often provide one. You've got to be different.

And Pepsi took advantage of its sweeter taste to challenge Coke in the hotly contested cola market. At the same time, Burger King was making progress against McDonald's with its "broiling, not frying" attack.

There are those who would say that a well-thought-out marketing plan always includes a section on the competition. Indeed it does. Usually toward the back of the plan in a section entitled "Competitive Evaluation." The major part of the plan usually spells out the marketplace, its various segments, and a myriad of customer research statistics carefully gleaned from endless focus groups, test panels and concept and market tests.

The marketing plan of the future

In the marketing plan of the future, many more pages will be dedicated to the competition. This plan will carefully dissect each participant in the marketplace. It will develop a list of competitive weaknesses and strengths as well as a plan of action to either exploit or defend against them.

There might even come a day when this plan will contain a dossier on each of the competitors' key marketing

Military warfare.

Territory

In a military war, two or more armies fight for control of territory. In Iraq, for example, the United States and its allies are fighting insurgents for control of the country.

people which will include their favorite tactics and style of operation (not unlike the documents the Germans kept on Allied commanders in World War II).

What does all this portend for marketing people of the future?

It means they have to be prepared to wage marketing warfare. More and more, successful marketing campaigns will have to be planned like military campaigns.

Strategic planning will become more and more important. Companies will have to learn how to *attack* and to *flank* their competition, how to *defend* their positions, and how and when to wage *guerrilla* warfare. They will need better intelligence on how to anticipate competitive moves.

On the personal level, successful marketing people will have to exhibit many of the same virtues that make a great military general—courage, loyalty, and perserverance.

Maybe Clausewitz is right

Maybe marketing is war, where the competition is the enemy and the objective is to win the battle.

Is this quibbling over details? Not really. Compare the game of football with the profession of marketing.

The football team that scores the most points wins the game. The marketing team that makes the most sales wins the marketing game. So far they're equivalent.

But try to play football the way you would play a marketing game.

Let's insert a marketing manager into a football game and watch him or her identify the goal line as the place to score points, that is, make sales. Then watch as the marketing manager lines up the team and heads straight for the goal line with the ball.

You don't have to be a sports expert to know that the direct approach in football leads to certain disaster.

In football, you win by outwitting, outflanking, outplaying the other team. The points on the scoreboard are only a reflection of your ability to do these things.

In war, you win by outwitting, outflanking, and overpowering the enemy. The territory you take is only a reflection of your ability to do these things.

Why should marketing be any different?

Why do the hundreds of definitions of the marketing concept almost never mention the word *competition?* Or suggest the essential nature of the conflict?

The true nature of marketing today involves the conflict between corporations, not the satisfying of human needs and wants.

If human needs and wants get satisfied in the process of business competition, then it is in the public interest to let the competition continue. But let us not forget the essential nature of what marketing is all about.

In defense of marketing warfare

You might object to the direct application of military principles to marketing. War is horrible enough in wartime, people have told us, without extending it to peacetime.

Marketing warfare.

Customers

In a marketing war, two or more companies fight for control of customers. Unlike a military war, a marketing war is never over.

Marketing is the strategy and tactics a company uses to win the battle of the marketplace.

With the help of Karl von Clausewitz and many other great military thinkers, we offer a new definition of marketing.

Enron, WorldCom, Global Crossing, and Adelphia are the latest examples of companies that have sustained huge losses. The public is concerned with fraud in the higher corporate ranks, but the real problem is not fraud but fraudulent strategies. Enron, for example, made the classic military mistake of dividing its forces by diversifying into many different industries. Originally a pipeline company, Enron got into trading power, communications, and weather securities as well as the development, construction, and operation of power plants worldwide. Had Enron stayed focused on being a profitable pipeline company, there would have been no reason to cook the books.

And anyone who is opposed to the free enterprise system would probably also object to having the participants in the system practice the principles of marketing warfare. So be it.

Even people who defend the free enterprise system might think that marketing warfare is going too far. If you are one of those people, we would urge you to consider the results of the warfare analogy rather than the analogy itself.

A study of American business history of the past decade or so suggests that many of the appalling financial losses registered by companies like RCA, Xerox, Western Union, and others might have been avoided by the application of the principles of war. The study of warfare is not just a study of how to win. Equally as important is how not to lose.

The American economy has more to fear from unlimited and senseless corporate aggression than it has from the skilled competition of marketing gladiators in the art of war.

Free enterprise is marketing warfare. If you want to play in the free enterprise game, it seems to make sense to learn the principles first.

Keep the forces concentrated in an overpowering mass. The fundamental idea. Always to be aimed at before all and as far as possible.
Karl von Clausewitz

2500 years of war

If marketing is war, let us make the most of us. Let us start by studying the history of war itself. And there is a lot of it to study.

According to Will and Ariel Durant, in the last 3438 years of recorded history, only 268 have seen no war. Much of early history is devoted to detailed chronicles of successful military campaigns and battles.

Before the birth of Jesus Christ, professional armies led by professional soldiers were meeting on battlefields around the world. Out of innumerable clashes between opposing armies, the principles of military strategy have been refined and perfected.

Marathon: 490 B.C.

At Marathon 15,000 Persians (from the area now called Iran) landed at the Bay of Marathon, northeast of Athens, where they faced 11,000 Athenians. Numerically weaker,

The Greek phalanx was a revolutionary concept that allowed individual warriors to operate in unison. In business, the same concept is known as "focus" and is a powerful way to create a marketing breakthrough.

the Greeks had one big advantage, the phalanx. Each Greek soldier held his shield so that it overlapped that of his neighbor, protecting half of himself and half of the man on his left.

The phalanx was more than a match for the Persians, who were used to one-on-one combat. Six thousand Persians fell as opposed to only 200 Athenians in this early-day version of the classic Hertz-vs.-Avis conflict.

At Marathon, the military tactics of working in unison and keeping the forces concentrated were firmly established.

Of course, we remember the event today because of the heroics of Pheidippides, the soldier who ran 22 miles to Athens with the news. "Rejoice! We conquer!" he blurted on his arrival—and promptly fell dead.

Nowadays our marathon runners go 26 miles, 365 yards. But, of course, they don't have to fight the Persians before starting the race.

Arbela: 331 B.C.

One hundred and fifty years later saw the rise of Alexander the Great. An early-day Thomas Watson, Alexander was a student of Aristotle and reader of Homer. He was both brave and cautious.

After victories on the Danube, Alexander hurried home to find trouble again brewing with the Persians under Darius. For 300 talents, Darius had hired Demosthenes, one of the first advertising agents, to spread false rumors that Alexander's army had perished.

After years of maneuvering, the decisive confrontation took place at Arbela in 331 B.C. So well documented are most military battles that even today, more than 2300 years later, we have the order of battle of both armies. (Will any Procter & Gamble marketing plan survive until the forty-third century?)

Darius arranged his forces in the conventional way, with 15 elephants and 200 chariots up front. Alexander was more creative. The key to Alexander's success was the use of cavalry on both flanks, a formation that was to be used in one form or another for the next 2000 years. The battle started with a "wing" attack by the right flank of Alexander's army led by the cavalry. The maneuver encouraged the Persians to attack Alexander's left flank, whereupon Alexander wheeled his mobile cavalry behind his center and used them to break through the Persians on the right.

Alexander achieved his greatest victory and became a king of kings with strategy that twentieth century military thinkers like B. H. Liddell Hart would call "the theory of the indirect approach."

A successful army, says Liddell Hart, operates on "the line of least expectation."

Like many great military commanders, Alexander the Great always led from the front and, as a result, was wounded many times. The major advantage of being in the center of the action is the ability to change tactics almost instantly. At Arbela, he led his mobile cavalry around the Persians' flank to great effect. In marketing as in warfare, the ability to shift your forces rapidly is often the key to victory.

Metaurus: 207 B.C.

The next military power to make a name for itself was Rome. The Romans proved their effectiveness as a fighting force along the river Metaurus in 207 B.C.

Carthaginian armies (from the area now known as Tripoli) were ravaging Italy. Led by the two "H" brothers

(Hannibal in the south and Hasdrubal in the north), the Carthaginians employed elephants to lead the charge, a forerunner of twentieth century armored warfare.

But it was a mistake for the "H" boys to divide their forces, and Nero (the general, not the violinist) would teach them the classic military principle of *keeping the forces concentrated in an overpowering mass.*

Nero first started south in the direction of Hannibal, but at nightfall he turned around and headed north. After one of the toughest forced marches in history, Nero joined Roman generals Porcius and Livius, who were facing Hannibal's brother Hasdrubal.

The battle itself was a replay of Arbela. Nero wheeled his forces from the right flank around Hasdrubal on the left flank. The charge was as successful as it was unexpected. And Nero gained a victory almost unrivaled in military annals.

But the press loves losers, not winners. So today we remember the misdeeds of his namesake, the Emperor Nero, who reigned 250 years later.

Even Hannibal and his elephants are more famous than Nero. In the words of the trade, "Winners tell jokes, losers hold press conferences."

Hastings: 1066

Skipping a thousand or so years, we come to the little English town of Hastings where the Normans under William (shortly to be known as William the Conqueror) were to change the course of history. Arrayed against the Normans were King Harold and his Saxons.

What elephants have in strength, they lack in nimbleness. At Metaurus, Nero skillfully maneuvered his Roman forces to defeat Hasdrubal and his elephants.

As in most battles, marketing as well as military, Hastings was a series of small successes and small reverses for both sides. Then William made a critical decision. He decided that Harold himself, a great personal leader, ought to be the key objective of the Norman attack.

So William assigned 20 Norman knights to break through the Saxon lines and get Harold. (Today we would send 20 lawyers armed with 5-year contracts.) Four Norman knights made it and promptly dispatched poor Harold.

William was right. When they saw their king had perished, the Saxon defense collapsed and William won his victory.

A section of the 230-foot-long Bayeux Tapestry shows Norman knights attacking King Harold at the battle of Hastings.

Crecy: 1346

But war is like business. It's never one-sided. At Crecy in 1346, the English got even with the French.

Key to Edward III's victory was the English longbow, a technological development not unlike a new product breakthrough in a marketing war. With the longbow—the machine gun of the fourteenth century—infantry and archers for the first time could stand up to mounted knights (the kind who did in poor Harold).

But the longbow, which could be fired six times faster than a crossbow, required skill and training to operate. With a 100-pound pull and a range of 200 yards, it took 6 years to become a full-fledged archer.

Which is why in Olde England archery practice on Sunday was compulsory. Church wasn't.

In military history, there were few technological developments as revolutionary as the English longbow. It enabled the English to dominate warfare for decades.

Only a handful of military battles have been decided by a superior weapon, and Agincourt was one of them. The same is true of marketing. Yet marketing people often mistake a minor technological advantage for a "longbow" and blithely sail out to do battle with an entrenched competitor, with the usual dismal results.

(Sixty-nine years later, at Agincourt in 1415, the French still hadn't learned the lesson. Here 5500 English troops defeated 20,000 French. Once again, the longbow was more than a match for mounted knights.)

Is it possible in *marketing* war to go head to head against a superior competitor?

Yes, but you need a longbow. Xerography, for example, in the case of the Haloid Company. The Land camera in the case of Polaroid.

Quebec: 1759

At Quebec in 1759, the French again came up short—as the English under James Wolfe took the "line of least expectation." The infantry went down the river behind Quebec and climbed the cliffs that were "impossible to climb" up to the Plains of Abraham.

In a marketing war, as in a military one, the "best" approach is not necessarily the most direct one. Ask yourself which approach is most likely to undermine the competitor's position.

Unfortunately, James Wolfe didn't live to enjoy the fruits of his famous victory. For that matter, neither did his opponent, the Marquis Louis Joseph de Montcalm—a reminder that in warfare, both military and marketing, there are always casualties.

On both sides.

Quebec is another example of a successful flanking attack. English infantry went down the river, climbed the cliffs, and surprised the French from behind.

Bunker Hill: 1775

Just 16 years later, war came a little closer to home. At Bunker Hill outside of Boston occurred the most famous battle of our own Revolutionary War.

It's a sad commentary on our knowledge of military history that the average American cannot tell you (1) which hill the battle of Bunker Hill was fought on and (2) which side won.

Dug in at the top of Breed's Hill, some distance away from Bunker Hill, were a thousand Americans under William "Don't Fire Till You See the Whites of Their Eyes" Prescott. At three in the afternoon, 3000 British troops under General William Howe started up the hill. The Americans held their fire until the Redcoats were 50 yards away.

It was carnage. As all frontal assaults against well-entrenched competition usually are. British losses were appalling. More than a thousand casualties out of the 3000 men engaged.

Who won? The British, of course. Outnumbered 3 to 1, the Americans were finally overrun. There were just too many white eyes and too many red coats.

After suffering appalling casualties in a direct assault, British forces finally took Breed's Hill, a battle known today as the Battle of Bunker Hill.

Trenton: 1776

Of course, everyone knows about the battle of Trenton in 1776. How George Washington crossed the Delaware on Christmas night and beat a superior force of Hessian soldiers. Right?

Wrong. Actually, Washington's forces outnumbered the Hessians (2000 to 1500). It was a combination of surprise plus superior numbers that won the day. Or rather, the night.

In marketing, too, never underestimate what Clausewitz calls the principle of force. The victory usually

By combining superior force with the element of surprise, George Washington achieved his most famous victory. When you can do that in a marketing war, victory is almost always assured.

Napoleon Bonaparte was perhaps history's most brilliant military strategist. The places he chose to do battle and the way he arrayed his forces were always dependent on careful assessments of his enemies' positions. Marketing people should do the same. Studying the enemy in great detail should be the first step in developing an effective marketing strategy.

belongs to the larger army. "God," said Napoleon Bonaparte, "is on the side of the big battalions."

Austerlitz: 1805

But at Austerlitz in 1805, perhaps Napoleon's biggest military success, he didn't have the big battalions.

What he did have was maneuverability. He tempted the Austrian-Russian alliance to attack his right flank. Then he maneuvered his left flank to strike at the enemy's weakened center.

The result was almost total victory. Rapidity of movement was the key to Napoleon's success. His troops, he claimed, could march 2 miles to the enemy's 1. "I may lose a battle," said Napoleon, "but I shall never lose a minute."

What about marketing? How many minutes, hours, days, and even weeks are lost in planning, in researching, in test marketing? Precious time often wasted. And the result: another defeat snatched from the jaws of victory.

(At Borodino in 1812, Napoleon forgot the lessons of Austerlitz. Against the advice of his aides, he threw his superior forces in a frontal assault against the Russians. Thirty thousand French troops died before the enemy melted away into the snow, a tableau that would be repeated by the forces of Adolph Hitler more than a century later.)

Waterloo: 1815

The end came 3 years later at the little Belgian village of Waterloo where Arthur Wellesley, the Duke of Wellington, blocked Napoleon's return to glory.

At Waterloo, Napoleon actually had a slight superiority in numbers: 74,000 men versus Wellington's 67,000. But Napoleon was on the offense, and Wellington could afford to wait. Napoleon knew he had to attack before the Prussians arrived to reinforce the Englishman and his allies.

Clausewitz's second principle of warfare is the superiority of the defense. A well-established defensive position is extremely strong and very difficult to overcome.

(So this year we predict that Chevrolet will be the largest-selling car, Crest will be the largest-selling toothpaste, and McDonald's the biggest fast-food company—regardless of what the competition does and how much money it spends.)

At 7:30 p.m., in the gathering darkness of June 18, 1815, Napoleon, in a final act of daring, ordered a frontal assault against the British center by 10 battalions of his Imperial Guards. *"De l'audace et toujours de l'audace."* (Audacity, always audacity.)

"Bonaparte used his last reserve," says Clausewitz, "in an effort to retrieve a battle which was past being retrieved. He spent his last farthing and then, as a beggar, abandoned both the battlefield and his crown."

What does Napoleon at Waterloo suggest to American Motors in Detroit?

Should they get out of the passenger car business while they still have a profitable Jeep business to fall back on?

"Capitulation is not a disgrace," says Clausewitz. "A general can no more entertain the idea of fighting to the last man than a good chess player would consider playing an obviously lost game."

Christopher Plummer as Wellington and Rod Steiger as Napoleon starred in the film *Waterloo*. Naturally, the loser, Rod Steiger, gets top billing. In spite of Napoleon's brilliance, at Waterloo and at so many other battles in military history, the defense prevailed. Note our comments about American Motors. After years of losses trying to attack the leaders, the company was finally sold to Chrysler, which proceeded to dump all the American Motors brands except Jeep. What's baffling is why American Motors didn't do that in the first place. As it turned out, the sport-utility vehicle market, pioneered by Jeep, became the largest, most profitable part of the automobile business. Dumping your losers and focusing on your winners is almost always a good strategy.

Balaclava: 1854

At Balaclava, the English under Lord Raglan faced the Russians under . . . who knows? Remember, winners are anonymous. (Who's president of General Motors? Or Procter & Gamble?)

At Balaclava occurred the world's most famous charge and the world's most effective charge.

The famous one, "The Charge of the Light Brigade," was a disaster. Straight into the guns of a superior force, Lord Cardigan led his famous 600, who were instantly routed with enormous losses.

The effective one, "The Charge of the Heavy Brigade," had occurred that same morning. It was the failure of the light brigade to follow up the success of the heavy brigade that led Raglan (the sleeve) to order Cardigan (the sweater) into action, an order misinterpreted with catastrophic results.

The Charge of the Light Brigade at Balaclava was a mistake, the result of misinterpreting an order. Yet the same scenario occurs in marketing almost every day of the week: an inferior force charges head-on against a superior enemy. What folly.

Gettysburg: 1863

History repeats itself. Only the names change. At Gettysburg in 1863, it was Robert E. Lee versus . . .

Well, do you remember the winning general's name? No, it wasn't Ulysses S. Grant.

It was George G. Meade—another in a long line of anonymous winners.

Hundreds of books have been written about this decisive battle of the Civil War. What if Lee had moved sooner? What if Pickett had delayed his charge? Yet look at the numbers. Lee had 75,000 men. Meade had 88,000 men.

Fame and fortune are not always linked. In marketing as well as in warfare, we tend to celebrate the losers rather than the winners—Napoleon Bonaparte, Robert E. Lee, and Carly Fiorina. (Everybody knows who Robert E. Lee was. That strange-looking man on the left is George G. Meade, the winning general at Gettysburg.)

So you don't have to read all those books to find out why the North won and the South lost. The first principle of warfare should have told you.

The principle of force is the "fundamental idea." "Always to be aimed at before all and as far as possible," says Clausewitz. "The greatest possible number of troops should be brought into action at the decisive point."

Clausewitz studied all the military battles of recorded history and found only two where the victory went to the side inferior in numbers by a factor of more than two to one. The vast majority of the time, the larger force prevailed.

The difference between our singing "Dixie" or "The Star Spangled Banner" at the ball game was just 13,000 men.

The Somme: 1916

The "war to end all war" began with the introduction of a deadly new weapon, the machine gun. Once again, a technological development strengthened the side of the defense (as television did in the marketing arena of the fifties and sixties).

The introduction of the machine gun changed the nature of warfare. Its defensive power made conventional infantry attacks almost impossible, a lesson learned by the allies at the river Somme. In the 1950s, television changed the nature of the marketing game, as did the Internet four decades later.

Nowhere was this point made more forcefully than along the river Somme in 1916. On July 1, after a week of artillery preparation, English and French troops came out of their trenches and advanced on a broad front—only to meet German machine-gun fire.

Allied casualties on the first day alone were 50,000. And the battle went on for 140 days. Slaughter on a scale never seen before or since.

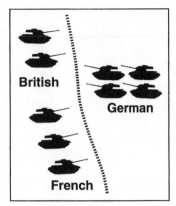

At the start of the Battle of France, the British and French actually had more tanks than the Germans (3,142 for the Allies and 2,580 for the Germans). But the Germans concentrated their panzer divisions and achieved a breakthrough at Sedan. "Deep penetration on a narrow front" became the accepted military mantra, a concept that marketers should also adopt.

And the gain purchased by the blood-soaked mud of the Somme? Just 5 miles.

(The following year at Cambrai, the British unveiled the tank, a technological development whose significance would not be appreciated until two decades later. The first day that tanks went into action, they advanced as far as 5 miles, as much as all of the infantry attacks did on the Somme. Unfortunately, the gain was not consolidated by infantry, and the British proceeded to lose the ground just as rapidly.)

Sedan: 1940

Your competitors often appreciate what you do more than your friends do. What the English market-tested at Cambrai in 1917 played a major role at Sedan in the forest of Ardennes in 1940.

In this classic battle of modern times, Von Rundstedt's panzer columns struck at the weak link of the Allied defenses, in between the French Maginot Line to the south and the British Expeditionary Forces to the north.

"You can't operate tanks in the Ardennes," said French military experts, presumably descendants of the same experts who thought the cliffs at Quebec were unclimbable.

As the Germans rolled on, the English wrote off the battle of France and prepared for the battle of Britain.

England's biggest ally was the English Channel, which forced the Germans to compete in the air. In their home skies, Hawker Hurricanes and Supermarine Spitfires were more than a match for Goering's Messerschmidts.

A few years later, the secret weapon of most successful wars, superiority of numbers, appeared on the scene with the arrival of the U.S. Army and General Dwight D. Eisenhower.

If ever a man personified the similarities between business and warfare, it was the good General Eisenhower. He worked in an office. He had an "in" and an "out" box. He had a secretary.

His language was the language of big business. "Do not needlessly endanger your lives," the general cautioned his troops poised for the invasion of Europe, "until I give you the signal."

We know the results of that invasion. Once again, we won a military battle and lost a marketing one as our former enemies, the Germans and the Japanese, outmaneuvered us on the marketing battlegrounds of the world.

And who will win the marketing wars of the eighties and the nineties? The marketing generals who have best learned the lessons of military history; the marketing generals who have learned to plan like Alexander the Great, maneuver like Napoleon Bonaparte, and fight like George S. Patton.

Except for the uniform, it would be hard to distinguish a military leader from a business leader. "The war will end," quipped Field Marshall Bernard Montgomery, "when the warring parties run out of paper."

The greatest possible number of troops should be brought into action at the decisive point. Karl von Clausewitz

2 The principle of force

How many times have you heard company people say it's easier to get to the top than to stay there?

Forget it. That's a myth created by people who are more interested in the study of sociology than they are in recognizing the realities of business competition.

It's far easier to stay on top than to get there. The leader, the king of the hill, can take advantage of the principle of force.

No other principle of warfare is as fundamental as the principle of force. The law of the jungle. The big fish eat the small fish. The big company beats the small company.

It was Civil War General Nathan Bedford Forrest who best expressed the essential philosophy of war: "Get there firstest with the mostest."

The mathematics of a firefight

When you examine the mathematics of a firefight, it's easy to see why the big company usually wins. Let's say that the Red squad with nine soldiers meets a Blue squad with six. Red has a 50 percent numerical superiority over the Blue.

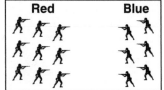

At the start of this firefight, the Red force outnumbers the Blue force 9 to 6.

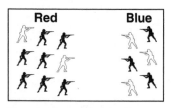

After the first volley, the Red force outnumbers the Blue force 7 to 3.

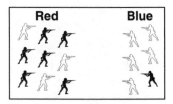

After the second volley, the Red force outnumbers the Blue force 6 to 1.

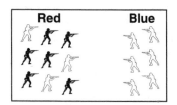

After the third volley, the Blue force is wiped out.

9 versus 6. Or it could be 90 versus 60 or 9000 versus 6000. It makes no difference what the numbers are, the principle is the same.

Let's also say that, on the average, one out of every three shots will inflict a casualty.

After the first volley, the situation will have changed drastically. Instead of a 9 to 6 advantage, Red would have a 7 to 3 advantage. From a 50 percent superiority in force to a more than 100 percent superiority.

The same deadly multiplication effect continues with the passage of time.

After the second volley, the score would be 6 to 1 in favor of Red.

After the third volley, Blue would be wiped out completely.

Notice how the casualties were divided between the two sides. The superior force (Red) suffered only half the casualties of the inferior force (Blue).

This result may be just the opposite of what you have been led to believe by all those Hollywood movies—the handful of marines decimating a company of Japanese before the marines are finally overrun.

In real life it's different. What happens when a Volkswagen Beetle hits a GMC bus in a head-on collision? You wind up with a few scratches on the bumper of the bus and a very thin German pancake. (The bigger you are, the harder they fall.)

The two vehicles have exchanged momentum. It's a basic law of physics. The larger, heavier vehicle sustains less damage than the smaller, lighter force.

There's no secret to why the Allies won World War II

in Europe. Where the Germans had two soldiers, we had four. Where they had four, we had eight. The skill and experience of an enemy who had practically invented modern warfare and the leadership of men like Rommel and Von Rundstedt could not change the mathematics of the battleground.

In the military, the numbers are so important that most armies have an intelligence branch known as the order of battle. It informs commanders of the size, location, and nature of the opposing force. (The case of General William C. Westmoreland against CBS was based on whether order of battle documents in the Vietnam war were falsified or not.)

The mathematics of a marketing melee

When two companies go head to head, the same principle applies. God smiles on the larger sales force.

Given a virgin territory, the company with the larger sales force is likely to wind up with the larger share of the market.

Once the market is divided up, the company with the larger share is likely to continue to take business away from the smaller company.

The bigger company can afford a bigger advertising budget, a bigger research department, more sales outlets, etc. No wonder the rich get richer and the poor get poorer.

Is there no future for the small competitor? Of course there is, which is one reason why this book was written. (General Motors, General Electric, and IBM don't need to study Clausewitz to be successful.)

ROMMEL
THE DESERT FOX
The classic biography of the legendary leader of Germany's Afrika Korps

"If this were a general instead of a book, it would rate five stars."—*Chicago Sunday Tribune*
DESMOND YOUNG

Erwin Rommel, also known as the Desert Fox, was a brilliant field commander in North Africa. He later took part in the attempt to assassinate Hitler, which unfortunately failed and cost him his life.

In Monroe, Michigan, is a statue of General George Armstrong Custer, a man who graduated last in his class at West Point and who, by dividing his forces, was responsible for the total loss of his regiment at Little Big Horn. Stupidity has its rewards, but unfortunately they often come after you're dead.

But smaller companies with smaller market shares do need to think like field commanders. They must keep in mind the first principle of warfare, the principle of force, be it military or marketing. "The art of war with a numerically inferior army," said Napoleon, "consists in always having larger forces than the enemy at the point which is to be attacked or defended."

Custer could have become one of our nation's most famous heroes if he could have gotten the Sioux to attack over the hill one at a time.

Military generals know the importance of the principle of force. That's why they spend so much time studying the order of battle of an opposing force. For purposes of morale, however, a general tries to fire up his troops by telling them what good soldiers they are and what great equipment they have.

"Now we have the finest food, equipment, the best spirit and the best men in the world," said George C. Scott in his role as General George S. Patton, Jr. "You know, by god, I actually pity those poor bastards we're going up against."

Many marketing generals do the same thing and fall victim to their own rhetoric. In particular they talk themselves into the "better people" or the "better product" fallacies.

The "better people" fallacy

It's easy enough to convince your own staff that better people will prevail, even against the odds. It's what they want to hear. And surely in a marketing war quality is a factor as well as quantity.

It is, but superiority of force is such an overwhelming advantage that it overcomes most quality differences.

We have no doubt that the poorest team in the National Football League could consistently beat the best team in the NFL if it could field 12 men against the opposition's 11.

In business, where the teams are much larger, your ability to amass a quality difference is much more difficult.

The clear-thinking marketing manager won't confuse the pep talk at a sales rally with the reality of the marketing arena. A good general never makes military strategy based on having better personnel. Nor should a marketing general. ("Our army," said Wellington, "is composed of the scum of the earth, the mere scum of the earth.")

Obviously you'd be in deep trouble inside your company if you used Wellington's words to describe your own army. Tell your people how terrific they are, but don't plan on winning the battle with superior personnel.

Count on winning the battle with a superior strategy.

Yet many companies cling deeply to the better people strategy. They're convinced they can recruit and hire substantially better people than the competition can, and that their better training programs can help them keep their "people" edge.

Any student of statistics would laugh at this belief. Sure, it's possible to put together a small cadre of superior people. But the larger the company, the more likely the average employee will be average.

What's wrong with hiring better people? Nothing, but the larger the company, the more likely it is that the company has "average" people. The difference between winners and losers is seldom people. It's almost always strategy. Management textbooks often argue that the first step in turning a company around is to hire better people and then let those people figure out a better strategy. But why would a superior person be attracted to a turn-around situation? A better approach is to first develop a better strategy, which will then attract better people.

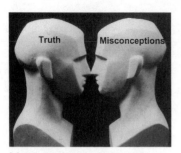

Many marketers believe that they have truth on their side and that their only problem is the need to change the misconceptions that exist in the prospect's mind.

And when it comes to the megacompanies, the possibility of assembling an intellectually superior team becomes statistically almost zero.

At last count, IBM had 369,545 employees, a number which is growing rapidly. On a one-to-one basis, there may be more white shirts at IBM but not more gray matter.

IBM is winning the computer war the Eisenhower way. Where the competition has 2, IBM has 4. Where the competition has 4, IBM has 8.

The "better product" fallacy

Another fallacy ingrained in the minds of most marketing managers is the belief that the better product will win the marketing battle.

Behind the thinking of many marketing managers is the thought that "truth will out."

In other words, if you have the "facts" on your side, it's only necessary to find a good advertising agency who can communicate those facts to the prospect and a good sales force who can close the sale.

We call this approach "inside-out thinking"—that somehow the advertising agency or the sales force can take the truth, as the company knows it, and use this truth to clear up the misconceptions that reside inside the mind of the prospect.

Don't be fooled. Misconceptions cannot easily be changed by an advertising or sales effort.

What is truth? Inside every human being is a little black box. When a human being is exposed to your advertising or sales claim, that person looks inside the box and says "That's right" or "That's wrong."

The single most wasteful thing you can do in marketing today is to try to change a human mind. Once a mind is made up, it's almost impossible to change.

What is truth? Truth is the perception that's inside the mind of the prospect. It may not be your truth, but it's the only truth you can work with. You have to accept that truth and then deal with it.

"If you're so smart, how come you're not rich?"

Even if you succeed in convincing the prospect that you have a better product, the prospect soon has second thoughts. "Hey, if your computer is better than IBM's, how come you're not the leader, like IBM is?"

Even if you get a few black boxes to go along with you, the owners of those black boxes soon let the unsold majority sway their judgment.

If you're so smart, how come you're not rich? That's a tough question to answer. In a marketing war you can't win just by being right.

There's the illusion, of course, that over the long run, the better product will win. But history, military and marketing, is written by the winners, not the losers.

Might is right. Winners always have the better product, and they're always available to say so.

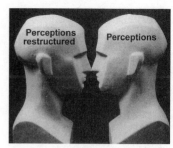

A better approach is to accept the prospect's perceptions as reality and then deal with them. Avis accepted the fact that it was No. 2 in the mind of the car rental prospect and then dealt with that perception by saying: "Avis is only No. 2 in rent a cars, so why go with us? We try harder."

The defensive form of war is in itself stronger than the offense.
Karl von Clausewitz

3 The superiority of the defense

The second principle of Clausewitz is the superiority of the defense.

No military commander would seek out combat with the odds stacked against him. The rule of thumb is that an attacking force, to be successful, should have a superiority of at least 3 to 1 at the point of attack.

Yet how many marketing generals are all too willing to start an offensive war with totally insufficient force? Like Cardigan at Balaclava and Lee at Gettysburg, many marketing generals launch offensive attacks with advertising and marketing dollars that are insufficient by a factor of 2 to 1, 3 to 1, even 10 to 1. With the same predictable results.

In warfare and in marketing, the advantage is always with the defense.

The mathematics of a defensive firefight

In an open field a firefight between two squads is rapidly decided in favor of the larger unit.

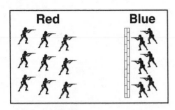

Red	Blue

The attackers (the Red force) outnumber the defenders (the Blue force) 9 to 6.

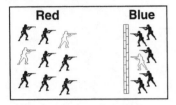

Red	Blue

After the first volley, the attackers still outnumber the defenders, but only 7 to 5.

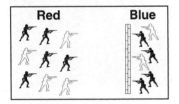

Red	Blue

After the second volley, the attackers outnumber the defenders 5 to 4.

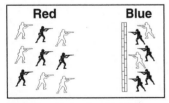

Red	Blue

After the third volley, the forces are even.

But what happens when one of the two squads is on defense? How does this change the mathematics of the situation?

Let's say a Red commander with a force of 9 soldiers meets a Blue commander with only 6 (a 50 percent superiority of force). But on this occasion the Blue force is on defense, say, in a trench or foxhole.

For a Blue soldier, the odds are still the same, 1 out of 3 shots, that he will hit one of the Red attackers.

What changes are the odds that a Red soldier will be able to hit one of the Blue forces, which now has the security of a defensive position? Instead of 1 out of 3, let's say the odds increase to 1 out of 9 shots.

(This corresponds to the difficulty of making "conquest" sales—that is, taking business away from an established competitor is usually much more difficult than getting business from a previously uncommitted prospect.)

After the first volley, the Red force still outnumbers the Blue, but by a margin of only 7 to 5. After the second volley, the margin is further reduced to 5 to 4. After the third volley the forces are the same, 4 to 4.

Red started the attack with a 50 percent superiority of force, but it's now even. At this point, the Red commander would presumably call off the attack since he no longer has superiority of numbers.

The fruit of victory

Throughout military history, defense has proved to be the stronger form of warfare. In the Korean war, America won in the South on defense and lost in the North on offense.

England lost in the Colonies on offense and won at Waterloo on defense.

Offense gets the glamour, but defense wins football games, as any NFL coach will hasten to tell you.

Why fight an offensive war at all if defense is so attractive? The paradox is the fruit of victory. If you can win a marketing battle and become the leading brand in a given category, you can enjoy that victory for a long time. Simply because you can now play defense, the stronger form of warfare.

A survey of 25 leading brands from the year 1923 proves this point. Sixty years later, 20 of those brands were still in first place. Four were in second place and one was in fifth place.

In six decades, only 5 out of 25 brands lost their leadership position. It's difficult to dethrone a king.

Ivory in soap, Campbell in soup, Coca-Cola in soft drinks. These represent strong marketing positions which can be taken only at great expense and with great skill and energy.

> **Eveready**
> **Kellogg's Corn Flakes**
> **Manhattan**
> **Ivory**
> **Palmolive**

It's now 80 years later, and still only 5 out of the 25 brands have lost their leadership. Eveready, for example, lost its lead in appliance batteries by being outflanked by Duracell.

Don't be a hero

The biggest mistake marketing people make is failing to appreciate the strength of a defensive position.

The glamour of offensive war and the thrill of victory makes the average marketing manager eager to pick up a lance and go charging off at the nearest entrenched competitor.

This is a classic example of an also-ran in mainframe computers attacking the leader head-on. Shortly after this advertising program ran, RCA announced that it was getting out of the computer business and wrote off $490 million.

They never learn. Years later, Sperry attacked IBM in personal computers. This didn't work, either. Eventually Sperry got out of the PC business.

Nothing in marketing is so pathetic as the charge of the light brigade. RCA and GE against IBM in computers. Exxon and Lanier against IBM in office automation. Western Union against everybody in electronic mail.

"Heroism" is a disease among too many marketing people eager to do or die for their company. If you approach the subject of marketing warfare looking for ways to cover yourself with marketing glory, you're reading the wrong book.

"Now I want you to remember that no bastard ever won a war by dying for his country," said George C. Scott in his Patton role. "He won it by making the other poor dumb bastard die for his country."

There are no heroes at IBM. No medals of honor awarded posthumously. Winners may be hard to admire, but as most losers will tell you, love is no consolation for having lost.

Friction favors the defense

One of the reasons the defensive form of warfare is so strong is the difficulty of launching a surprise attack.

"In theory," says Clausewitz, "surprise promises a great deal. In practice, it generally strikes fast by the friction of the whole machine."

In theory, the 1916 battle of the Somme was going to be a surprise attack. But after moving a million men into position and waiting a week for the artillery to do its job, the Allies were left with little surprise.

The larger the operation, the less the surprise. A small company might be able to surprise a big company with a new product. But Ford is unlikely to pull any fast ones on General Motors. The friction of the whole machine gets in the way.

When you look at case histories of leaders who were taken by surprise, you usually find they had ample warning. Leaders get overrun when they ignore those warnings or pooh-pooh the efforts of the competition.

In *Mein Kampf,* a book that sold some 10 million copies, Hitler told England and France exactly what he intended to do. A decade later he did it.

An attack takes time

An attacker in a military campaign not only tends to sacrifice surprise but also wastes time in bringing the forces into action. Because of logistics problems, it can be days or weeks before the full force of an attack is felt by a defender—time that can be enormously useful to the defense.

On D day, only 156,115 troops were put ashore on the Normandy beaches in spite of a massive effort. Because of transportation and supply problems, it took several months to build up Allied strength to the millions of troops necessary to ensure success.

In a marketing attack, transportation is usually not a problem. A company can deliver products to thousands of outlets in days.

The bottleneck is communication. Getting a marketing message across to millions of customers can take

Many of the tragedies of World War II, including the Holocaust, might have been prevented if the Allies had attacked Germany before its military buildup in the period from 1936 to 1939. Adolf Hitler's book *Mein Kampf* ("My Struggle") should have sent a chilling signal. Typical quote: "A thirty-centimeter shell has always hissed more loudly than a thousand Jewish newspaper vipers—so let them hiss!"

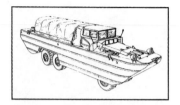

The landing craft that hit the beaches on D-day (June 6, 1944) were no surprise to the Germans. The only question was where the landings would take place. The Allies tried to bluff the enemy into thinking they would land at Calais when the actual invasion was going to take place in Normandy. The launch of the IBM PC, the first serious 16-bit business personal computer, in August 1981 was no surprise, either. We had heard rumors of such a product nearly a year in advance and tried to get our client, Digital Equipment, to preempt the category by launching a similar product well in advance of the IBM introduction. Digital Equipment refused to do so, a strategic mistake that cost the company dearly.

months or years. There is often plenty of time for the defender to blunt the attacker's sales message by undercutting it in one form or another.

But to take advantage of time, the defender has to remain alert to potential threats from any direction.

Some statesmen and generals try to avoid the decisive battle. History has destroyed this illusion.   Karl von Clausewitz

4 The new era of competition

The most bloodthirsty language in the newspapers today is not found in the international pages. It's found on the business pages.

"We'll murder them."

"It's kill or be killed."

"This is a life-or-death struggle."

No, these are not the words of a leftist guerrilla or a right-wing dictator. These are typical quotes from three business leaders discussing forthcoming marketing campaigns.

The language of marketing has been borrowed from the military. We *launch* a marketing *campaign.* Hopefully, a *breakthrough* campaign.

We *promote* people to higher *positions.* In *divisions, companies, units.* We *report gains* and *losses.* Sometimes we *issue uniforms.*

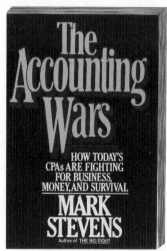

"War" has become a widely used metaphor for business conflicts, but unfortunately most authors are unfamiliar with the strategies and tactics of real warfare.

37

From time to time we go into the *field* to *inspect* those uniforms and *review* the progress of the *troops*. We have even been known to *pull rank*.

Up till now, it's only the language that has been borrowed from the military, not the strategic thinking behind the language.

Marketing warfare is an attempt to apply military thinking to marketing problems.

Marketing, as a scientific discipline, is less than 100 years old. Marketing is long on "seat of the pants" thinking and short on theory. Military theory can help bridge the gap.

The headline wars

If you've been reading *Business Week, Forbes,* or *Fortune,* you've probably had your fill of military language. The *beer war,* the *cola war,* and the *hamburger war* are recent examples of journalistic militarism.

But underneath the headlines, the writers totally ignore the most elementary of military principles.

"New Xerox push in the office," said a recent headline in *The New York Times.* "Seeks lead in automation," said the subhead.

If Denmark invaded West Germany, a country 12 times its size, the press would express shock and incredulity.

Lead in automation? Xerox, a company with less than $2 billion in annual sales of office automation products, going up against IBM, a company with more than $40 billion?

Xerox attacked IBM head-on with a line of mainframe computers, a strategy that cost Xerox billions of dollars in losses.

There are many more examples of the semantic smoke without the strategic fire.

"National Semiconductor is crossing the Rubicon," said President Charles E. Sporck in the headline of an advertisement announcing the company's line of micro- and minicomputers.

When Julius Caesar crossed the real Rubicon in 49 B.C., he did so with a full legion of men (with two more in reserve). So awesome was Caesar's strength that his opponent, Pompey, promptly decided to evacuate Italy.

Where are Sporck's legions? Will IBM give up so quickly? You don't have to be a military genius to know that this semi-invasion won't be very successful.

Predictions or propaganda?

When Coca-Cola announced its new, sweeter formula, it also confidently predicted a 1 percent gain in market share over each of the next 3 years. Was this a prediction or just propaganda? If it was meant to be propaganda, it missed the mark. No military commander in his right mind gives a timetable for victory.

"I shall return," said Douglas MacArthur when he left the Phillippines in March 1942. If he had added "by the end of the year," his reputation would have been seriously dampened by the time he waded ashore in 1944. Unkept promises undermine morale. Marketing promises should be as vague as political ones. Otherwise, they will erode the effectiveness of your forces.

National Semiconductor
The Sight & Sound of Information

To get into the personal computer business, National Semiconductor bought Cyrix Corporation for $550 million. Less than two years later, it got out of the business and retreated back across the Rubicon, taking a charge of several hundred million dollars. The company, however, survived, and today it avoids competing with the computer manufacturers (Dell and Hewlett-Packard) and the big chip makers (Intel and AMD). National Semiconductor is a specialist in analog and mixed-signal chips with healthy sales ($2 billion last year) and a healthy profit margin (14 percent). Specialists can survive and prosper in almost any market.

When Hitler promised to take Stalingrad and failed, he lost more than his military reputation. He also lost his "master of propaganda" image.

The reality of marketing conflict

Rhetoric aside, it's clear that marketing is entering a new era, an era that will make the sixties and seventies look like a Sunday school picnic. Competition is getting brutal. The name of the game has become "taking business away from somebody else."

As companies experiment with different ways to increase sales, they are turning more and more to warfare strategies in general.

But aggressiveness alone is not the mark of a good military strategy. Especially aggressiveness as represented by the "more" school of management. More products, more sales people, more advertising, more hard work.

Especially more hard work. Somehow we feel better about success if we have to work hard to achieve it. So we schedule more meetings, more reports, more memos, more management reviews.

Yet military history teaches the reverse. A single-minded commitment to winning the battle on effort alone usually dissolves into defeat. From the trenches of World War I to the streets of Stalingrad in World War II, the military commander that lets his armies get bogged down in a hand-to-hand slugging match is usually defeated.

The dogged determination of Xerox to make it in the office automation market is not a sign of future success. It's a mark of futility.

Much better are quick, lightninglike strokes that depend more on timing than muscle. (What the Germans call *blitzkrieg*.) Not that muscle, or the principle of force, is not important. Far from it. But unless an attack is properly planned, you throw away your advantage if you let the battle degenerate into a war of attrition.

Whenever you hear your commander say "We have to redouble our efforts," you know you're listening to a loser talk. The lights don't need to burn late in places like Armonk. IBM wins by thinking smarter, not longer.

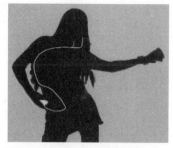

The enormous success of Apple's iPod demonstrates the power of taking "the line of least expectation." Apple's enemies are Microsoft and the personal computer manufacturers using the Windows operating system. Rather than launching a direct assault on an entrenched competitor, Apple put the bulk of its resources into a flanking attack with the iPod, the first hard-drive MP3 player. Furthermore, the product launch was coordinated with the introduction of a Web site selling iTunes, a strategy reminiscent of the air-and-armor coordination of a military attack.

It is from the character of our adversary's position that we can draw conclusions as to his designs and will therefore act accordingly.

Karl von Clausewitz

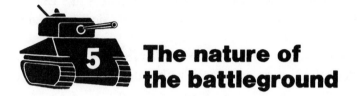

5 The nature of the battleground

In a military battle the terrain is so important that a battle is invariably named after its geographic location.

The Plain of Marathon, the river Metaurus, the village of Waterloo, a town named Gettysburg, a hill named Bunker, a mountain called Cassino.

In a marketing battle, the terrain is important too. But the question is "Where." Where is the terrain? Where are marketing battles being fought?

A mean and ugly place

In this book you'll read about the value of holding the marketing "high ground" and the need to avoid a "well-entrenched" competitor. Where is the high ground? Where are the trenches?

If you want to go out and do battle with your competitors, it's helpful to know where to go.

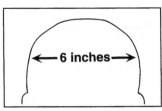

←— 6 inches —→

Marketing is fought on a battleground six inches wide, the mind of the prospect. This is a critical concept in understanding the essence of marketing. You don't win with a better product. You win with a better perception.

We published 27 issues of a marketing newsletter entitled Battleground until we got bored with it. The objective was to analyze various marketing situations from a military point of view. With the raft of good cases histories available today, we should have continued to publish the newsletter.

Marketing battles are not fought in the customer's office or in the supermarkets or the drugstores of America. Those are only distribution points for the merchandise whose brand selection is decided elsewhere.

Marketing battles are not fought in places like Dallas, Detroit, or Denver. At least not in the physical sense of a city or a region.

Marketing battles are fought in a mean and ugly place. A place that's dark and damp with much unexplored territory and deep pitfalls to trap the unwary.

Marketing battles are fought inside the mind. Inside your own mind and inside the mind of your prospects, every day of the week.

The mind is the battleground. A terrain that is tricky and difficult to understand.

The entire battleground is just 6 inches wide. This is where the marketing war takes place. You try to outmaneuver and outfight your competitors on a mental mountain about the size of a canteloupe.

A marketing war is a totally intellectual war with a battleground that no one has ever seen. It can only be imagined in the mind, which makes marketing warfare one of the most difficult disciplines to learn.

Mapping the mind

A good general carefully studies the terrain before the battle. Every hill, every mountain, every river is analyzed for its defensive or offensive possibilities.

A good general also studies the enemy's position. Hopefully, the exact location and strength of each unit is plotted on a map and studied before the battle begins. The best surprise is no surprise. What a commander hopes to avoid at all costs is a surprise attack from an unexpected direction.

In a marketing war, reconnaissance is extraordinarily difficult. How do you see inside a human mind to find out what the terrain looks like and what strong points the enemy holds?

One way to reconnoiter the human mind is to use marketing research. But not in the traditional way of asking customers what they want to buy. That's yesterday's approach.

What you're trying to find out is what positions are held by what companies. Who owns the high ground?

Done correctly, you can contour the mind of the average prospect to produce a map that is just as useful to a marketing general as the Michelin maps that Patton carried across Europe.

Mapping the mental battleground can give you an enormous advantage. Most of your competitors won't even know where the battle is being fought. They will be preoccupied with their own camp: their own products, their own sales force, their own plans.

In association with AMR International, we ran quite a few seminars on marketing warfare in cities like San Francisco and New York. Among our military speakers were General William C. Westmoreland, Admiral Elmo R. Zumwalt, and Major General George Smith Patton (son of the World War II general.)

Mountains in the mind

Any attempt to describe a human mind in physical terms is bound to be symbolic. Yet there are certain symbols used in both military and marketing operations that seem to be especially appropriate.

Few brands are stronger than Budweiser, which sits on top of Beer Mountain. "King of Beers" is a powerful metaphor for the Budweiser brand. Many have tried, but few brands have dented Budweiser's lock on the beer business.

In a military war, hills or mountains are usually considered strong positions, especially useful for defense. In a marketing war, management people often refer to strong positions as "high ground." So it seems appropriate to use the mountain as a key concept in marketing warfare.

But in warfare, a mountain can be either occupied or unoccupied. Tissue mountain, for example, is occupied by the brand Kleenex. Ketchup mountain is owned by Heinz. Computer mountain by IBM.

Some mountains are being strongly contested. Cola mountain is partially occupied by Coca-Cola, but is under heavy attack by Pepsi-Cola.

When a customer uses a brand name in place of a generic, you know the mountain in their mind is strongly held. When someone points to a box of Scott tissues and says, "Hand me a Kleenex," you know who owns the tissue mountain in that person's mind.

Segmentation is tearing up the terrain

Who owns the automobile mountain in the United States? Many years ago Ford did. But Ford got torn apart by the segmentation strategy of General Motors.

So today Chevrolet, Pontiac, Oldsmobile, and Buick each own different segments of the automotive mountain, with perhaps Cadillac in the strongest position as the owner of the high-priced luxury segment. (Today people will use the name Cadillac as a synonym for a high-quality product. "It's the Cadillac of television sets.") As a result of its five strong independent positions, General Motors owns the dominant share of the U.S. automotive market.

Monolithic mountains are being fought over and cut up into segments, each owned by a different warlord. This long-term trend is likely to continue well into the twenty-first century.

The original owner has a choice: extend or contract. Faced with an enemy that attempts to segment the market, a company can extend its forces to try to control the entire territory, or shrink them to protect home base.

The owner's instincts are usually wrong. Greed encourages a brand leader to extend its forces to try to control all segments. Too often everything is lost in an effort to protect a small portion of the mountain. As Frederick the Great once said, "He who attempts to defend everywhere defends nothing."

Is there no defense against a competitor who attempts to segment your mountain? Fortunately for the big companies of this world, there is. More on this strategy in the chapter on defensive warfare.

> **CREDIT RANKINGS OF G.M. AND FORD LOWERED TO JUNK**
>
> **WEAK SALES CITED BY S.&P.**

One reason General Motors is in trouble today is its strategic decision to defend every single segment of the automotive market. Small cars, compact cars, intermediates, luxury cars, sports cars, minivans, sport-utility vehicles, trucks—General Motors makes them all.

The first, the supreme, the most far-reaching act of judgment that the statesman and commander have to make is to establish the kind of war on which they are embarking; neither mistaking it for, nor trying to turn it into something that is alien to its nature.

Karl von Clausewitz

6 The strategic square

There is no one way to fight a marketing war. Rather there are four. And knowing which type of warfare to fight is the first and most important decision you can make.

Which type to fight depends on your position in a strategic square which is easy to construct for any industry.

As an example, let's take the U.S. automobile industry. It's a tightly knit, well-established industry. As a matter of fact, the last person to start an automobile company in this country and have it survive was Walter P. Chrysler in 1925.

So today we have the big four: General Motors, Ford, Chrysler, and American Motors. But if Clausewitz were alive today and got off the plane at Metro Airport in Detroit, he would take one look at the situation and immediately straighten everyone out.

It's not the big four. In terms of share of market, it's really the big one. General Motors gets 59 percent of the market.

General Motors	Ford
Chrysler	American Motors

The domestic automobile industry was often called "The Big Four."

General Motors	Ford
Chrysler	AM

In reality, the automobile industry was more like "The Big One-and-Three-Quarters," with General Motors as the dominant player.

Defensive	Offensive
Flanking	Guerrilla

Because of their relative sizes, General Motors should have practiced defensive warfare; Ford, offensive warfare; Chrysler, flanking warfare; and American Motors, guerrilla warfare.

All the others don't add up to the one of General Motors. In share of market, Ford has 26 percent of the U.S. market, Chrysler has 13 percent, and American Motors has 2 percent. Total for the little three: 41 percent.

Of course, this analysis neglects the imports which represent an additional 34 percent (equivalent to 25 percent of the total U.S. automobile market). Imports are important as these numbers indicate, but our purpose is not to analyze the industry in all its detail. Our purpose is to illustrate the four types of marketing warfare, using the traditional Detroit foursome as examples.

There are significant differences in strength between American Motors, Chrysler, Ford, and General Motors. Each company is half the size of the next larger company in the field. There is no parity in this league. It's as if a grade school, a high school, a college, and a professional football team were assembled in a four-team league. Is there any doubt who would win?

The game is more than winning. Of course, General Motors will put more points on the scoreboard. For the others, winning has other definitions.

For Ford, increasing its share of the market would represent a substantial victory.

For Chrysler, profitable survival would be enough to declare a victory.

For American Motors, survival would be enough.

In a given marketing situation, each company has different resources, different strengths, different goals. Is it any wonder that each company should have a different marketing strategy?

What type of warfare should General Motors, Ford, Chrysler, and American Motors wage? Let's look at the position of each company.

The type of warfare General Motors should wage

First, who are General Motors' competitors? There's the Justice Department, the Federal Trade Commission, the Security & Exchange Commission, and the U.S. Congress (both houses).

General Motors can't win by winning. If they wiped out one or more of their automotive competitors, the courts or the Congress would break them up. Witness what happened to that other big winner, the American Telephone and Telegraph Company. They were no match for Judge Greene and the Department of Justice.

General Motors can only win by not losing. General Motors should wage defensive warfare.

But defensive warfare should not be construed to mean a passive operation. "Defense in itself," says Clausewitz, "is a negative exercise, since it concentrates on resisting the intentions of the enemy rather than being occupied with our own."

Rather, good defensive warfare is offensive in nature with the clear objective of protecting a company's dominant share of market.

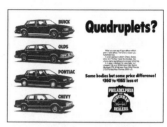

How the mighty have fallen. Today, General Motors is a company in trouble. The problem? GM destroyed the purity of its fighting forces. Its brands began to compete with one another rather than with the competition. The launch of Saturn, for example, undermined Chevrolet, its entry-level brand. Then, too, prospects often couldn't tell the difference between the various GM brands. In some cases, they were the same car with different nameplates. Here is how the Philadelphia Chevrolet dealer association tried to take advantage of the fact that a Pontiac, an Oldsmobile, and a Buick are just Chevrolets with higher price tags.

What Ford should do

Ford is a strong No. 2. Ford has the resources to launch offensive attacks. But who should they attack?

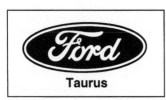

Taurus

Ford did attack General Motors, and very successfully, too. The point of the Ford attack was the Taurus, and it was directed at the heart of the General Motors line, its Chevrolet brand. While Chevrolet was introducing a variety of different sedans, Ford poured billions of dollars into developing one model, the Taurus. Thanks primarily to the Taurus, the Ford brand went on to outsell Chevrolet and still does today.

As Willie Sutton used to say, "I rob banks because that's where the money is." Ford should attack General Motors because that's where the market is.

It's easy to see mathematically why Ford should attack General Motors. If Ford could take 10 percent of General Motors' business, they would increase their own market share by 25 percent. If Ford should take 10 percent of American Motors, the effect on Ford's volume would be hard to measure.

The temptation is to prey on the weak rather than the strong—on the theory of "easy pickings." Yet the opposite is closer to the truth. The smaller the company, the harder it will fight to protect the small share it does own, with such tactics as price cuts, discounts, lengthened warranties. Never pick a fight with a wounded animal.

Ford's best strategy is to wage offensive warfare. They should launch offensive attacks against weak points in the General Motors line. How to find and exploit those weak points is the subject of another chapter.

What Chrysler should do

Old African proverb: When elephants fight, it's the ants that take a beating. Chrysler should avoid the battle between General Motors and Ford and launch flanking attacks.

This is exactly what Lee Iacocca has done. Some of his classic flanking attacks against the entire U.S. automotive industry include the "first" convertible, the first minivan, the first six-passenger front-wheel-drive car.

What Mr. Iacocca has accomplished is all the more brilliant when you realize where he was coming from. After 8 years at the top of Ford, he made an abrupt switch to Chrysler, helped along by a gentle push from Henry Ford II. What could have been expected is the grafting of a Ford strategy onto a Chrysler organization. Not so. Iacocca deserves the credit for developing a different strategy, much more appropriate to the situation he found at Chrysler.

How many marketing generals would have been able to do the same? Most of us would have tried to play the marketing game the way we had successfully played it in the past.

In retrospect, there was one Ford strategy that Iacocca could have used as a pattern for Chrysler. That was the successful flanking attack represented by the Mustang, the first two-passenger "personal" car. Iacocca personally developed the hot-selling car after selling a reluctant Henry Ford on the idea.

Lee Iacocca's leadership skills are often given the credit for Chrysler's turnaround. Even more important, in our opinion, were his strategic skills. In particular, the minivan was a master "flanking" stroke, the single most important decision that kept the Chrysler Corporation alive until Daimler-Benz came along to buy it.

What American Motors should do

What can you say about poor American Motors except head for the hills, put on your black pajamas, and become a guerrilla.

American Motors is too small to launch offensive attacks against General Motors. Even if initially successful, American Motors doesn't have enough dealers, enough manufacturing capacity, enough marketing muscle to sustain a marketing attack.

A brand that doesn't stand for anything is a brand that is worthless. The only brand owned by American Motors that stood for anything was Jeep. What if American Motors had renamed itself the Jeep Corporation and sold nothing but Jeeps at Jeep dealerships? Would the Jeep Corporation be a viable brand today? We think so. When Chrysler Corporation bought American Motors, Lee Iacocca threw out all the brands except for Jeep. What if Chrysler had renamed itself the American Motors Corporation and sold nothing but Jeeps, Chrysler minivans, and Dodge trucks? Three brands, three dominant automotive positions. Would the former Chrysler Corporation still be a viable company today instead of a division of DaimlerChrysler? We think so.

American Motors is too small to launch a flanking attack against the industry. Not too small to *start* a flanking attack as the company proved with the Nash Rambler. But too small to dominate the segment after being the first to launch the concept.

The only category that has been a consistent winner for American Motors is the Jeep. This is a classic guerrilla tactic. Find a segment big enough to be profitable for the guerrilla, but too small to be tempting to the leader.

The mountain in the mind

Let's review the battleground in the mind. The mountain, of course, is the high ground owned by the leader.

If you go through the mountain, then you are fighting an offensive marketing war. Hopefully, you'll find a valley or crevice that your troops can break through. But the battle is tough and often costly because the leader usually has the resources to make strong counterattacks.

If you come down the mountain to stop competitive attacks, then you are fighting a defensive marketing war. And the rule is, the best defense is a good offense.

If you go around the mountain, then you are fighting a flanking marketing war. This is usually the most effective and least expensive type of marketing operation to conduct. But opportunities for good flanking moves are becoming scarce in many product categories.

If you go under the mountain, you are fighting a guerrilla marketing war. You want to select a territory secure enough to defend. Or too small for the leader to bother with.

The statesman who, seeing war inevitable, hesitates to strike first is guilty of a crime against his country.   Karl von Clausewitz

7 Principles of defensive warfare

There are three basic principles of defensive marketing warfare. Each is easy to learn but difficult to put into practice. If you want to play a good game of defense, however, it will pay you to study each of the principles in detail.

Defensive principle No. 1

Only the market leader should consider playing defense. This might seem straightforward, but it's not.

We've never met a company that didn't consider itself a leader. But most companies base their leadership positions more on creative definitions than on market realities. Your company may be the leader "east of the Mississippi on Monday morning," but the customer doesn't care.

Companies don't create leaders—customers do. It's who the customer perceives as the leader that defines a true category leader.

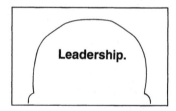

Leadership.

Leadership is a powerful motivating force only when it's in the consumer's mind. Power doesn't derive from actual market leadership, but from perceptual leadership.

Furthermore, we're talking about *the* leader, not *a* leader. There are many leaders in the computer industry, but only one IBM, the true leader in the mind of computer customers and prospects.

Then there are the pretenders to the throne. Some business people actually believe you can "will" your way to the top. They believe in the power of positive thinking. First, you have to convince yourself you're the leader before you can go out and convince others.

Torpedo the thought. Pretendership has no place in the development of a marketing strategy. It's one thing to engage in hyperbole for the benefit of the sales force. It's another thing to delude yourself into making a strategic error. A good marketing general must have a clear picture of the actual situation so that he or she can lead from truth. Fool the enemy, never fool yourself.

Defensive principle No. 2

The best defensive strategy is the courage to attack yourself.

Because of its leadership position, the defender owns a strong point in the mind of the prospect. The best way to improve your position is by constantly attacking it. In other words, you strengthen your position by introducing new products or services that obsolete your existing ones.

IBM is a master of the game. Every so often, IBM introduces a new line of mainframe computers with significant price/performance advantages over existing products.

Competition continually struggles trying to catch up. A moving target is harder to hit than a stationary one.

Gillette is another example. Gillette owned the wet-shaving market with a product called the Blue Blade and subsequently the Super Blue Blade.

The company was stunned when rival Wilkinson Sword beat it to the market in the early sixties with the stainless blade. Then in 1970 Wilkinson Sword followed with the bonded blade, a metal blade fused to plastic at the "optimum shaving angle." At that point Gillette got its act together and started to play a brilliant game of defensive warfare.

Shortly thereafter Gillette counterattacked with Trac II, the world's first double-bladed razor. The success of Trac II set the pattern for future Gillette strategy. "Two blades are better than one," said Gillette's advertising.

"Better than one Super Blue Blade," said the company's customers who promptly bought the new product instead of the old. (It's better to take business away from yourself than have someone else do it for you.)

Six years later, the company introduced Atra, the first adjustable double-bladed razor. Again, by implication the new product was better than the Trac II, the nonadjustable two-bladed razor.

Nor did Gillette hesitate to introduce Good News, an inexpensive disposable razor (with two blades, no less). This was an obvious attack against Bic, who was preparing to introduce its own disposable razor.

Good News was not good news for Gillette stockholders. The disposable cost more to make and sold for less than Gillette's refillable razor blades. So anyone buying a Good News blade rather than an Atra or Trac II was costing Gillette money.

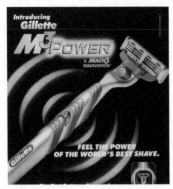

Gillette has continued its "attack yourself" strategy. Its most stunning success is the Mach 3 razor, which not only is highly profitable, but has captured a significant market share. Recently Gillette continued its defensive strategy by introducing the M3 Power battery-powered razor. (M3 Power is a much weaker name than Mach 3.)

But Good News was good marketing strategy. It blocked Bic from running away with the disposable portion of the market. Furthermore, Bic paid dearly for its modest share. Trade sources say Bic lost $25 million in its first 3 years in the disposable razor business.

Gillette continues its relentless strategy of attacking itself. Recently it introduced Pivot, the first adjustable disposable. This time, its own Good News product is the target.

Gillette has gradually increased its share of the wet-shaving market. Today it has some 65 percent of the business.

Attacking yourself may sacrifice short-term profits, but it has one fundamental benefit. It protects market share, the ultimate weapon in any marketing battle.

The reverse is also true. Any company that hesitates to attack itself usually loses market share and ultimately market leadership.

Recently, Schick struck back with the Quattro, the first four-bladed razor. So what will Gillette do next? Of course, introduce a five-bladed razor.

Defensive principle No. 3

Strong competitive moves should always be blocked.

Most companies have only one chance to win, but leaders have two. If a leader misses an opportunity to attack itself, the company can often recover by copying the competitive move. But the leader must move rapidly before the attacker gets established.

Many leaders refuse to block because their egos get in the way. Even worse, they knock the competitor's development until it's too late to save the situation.

Blocking works well for a leader because of the nature of the battleground. Remember, the war takes place inside the mind of the prospect. It takes time for an attacker to make an impression in the mind. Usually, there's time enough for the leader to cover.

The U.S. automobile industry illustrates this principle well. Says John DeLorean in the book *On a Clear Day You Can See General Motors:* "Even though Ford was superior to General Motors in product innovation during the time I was with GM and Chrysler surpassed it in technical innovation, neither firm made substantial cuts into GM's half of the market."

"GM had not produced a significant, major automotive innovation since the hydramatic automatic transmission (1939) and the hard-top body style (1949)," continues DeLorean, "Ford pioneered in practically every major new market while Chrysler produced the significant technical innovations, such as power steering, power brakes, electric windows and the alternator."

But who gets the credit for engineering excellence? General Motors, of course.

It's the flip side of the "truth will out" fallacy. The prospect also assumes that truth will out. Therefore, the prospect reasons that the market leader must have truth on its side, that is, the GM product is superior.

There is also the psychological pressure that benefits the leader. In a famous experiment by Solomon Asch of the University of Pennsylvania, many people were willing to go against the evidence of their own senses in order to go along with the majority.

When asked to match the length of a set of lines and confronted with a group that had been carefully briefed to give unanimously wrong answers, 37 percent of the subjects submitted to the misleading group opinion and also gave the wrong answers.

The power of the majority was indicated by the typical reaction in the Asch experiment: "To me it seems I'm right, but my reason tells me I'm wrong, because I doubt that so many people could be wrong and I alone right."

The fact is, many people pay more attention to the opinion of others than they do to their own. If everyone else is laughing in the theater, you assume the movie is funny. If no one else is laughing, you assume the movie is not funny. (That's why they put the laugh tracks on the TV situation comedies.)

Should a leader cover all bets or just the ones that are most likely to succeed? Obviously there's no point in covering downright silly ideas, but who's to judge? When the first Volkswagen Beetle arrived, it looked strange indeed. "The three most overrated things in America," went a typical Detroit joke, "are Southern cooking, home sex, and foreign cars."

Many companies have lived to regret instant put-downs like this. So today the watchword is more likely to be: "Let's monitor the situation and see what happens."

But that can be a dangerous tactic for a leader. Too often what happens, happens too fast. All of a sudden, it's too late to get into the new ball game.

Currently, disposables represent about 40 percent of the razor blade market. If Gillette had waited and let Bic dominate this market segment, Gillette's position would be much weaker today.

It's safer to overcover than to undercover. The stainless steel blade introduced by Wilkinson Sword never went anywhere, but Gillette covered anyway. The small cost was worth it. Call it insurance if you wish.

The battle for Migraine Mountain

That's our name for one of the classic blocking moves of all time. Not only did it totally smash a competitive move, but the covering move catapulted the brand to the position of the best-selling drugstore product in America.

What happened on Migraine Mountain documents the critical importance of timing. If you want to cover, you have to do it right away. If you wait, it may be too late.

The brand is Tylenol, an acetaminophen product marketed by Johnson & Johnson's McNeil Laboratories. Priced 50 percent higher than aspirin and promoted mainly to physicians and other health care specialists, Tylenol was headed up the sales charts.

The people at Bristol-Myers thought they saw an opportunity. So in June 1975 Bristol-Myers introduced Datril with the "same pain reliever, same safety as Tylenol."

The difference is the price, said Datril ads which quoted $2.85 as the price of 100 Tylenol tablets and $1.85 for Datril.

One of Bristol-Meyers' mistakes was to market-test the idea in its traditional test markets, Albany and Peoria. Any guess who was watching the test with eagle eyes?

Johnson & Johnson lowers the boom

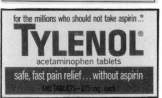

Tylenol's reaction to the Datril attack is a classic example of what a leader needs to do to protect its position. When Datril died, Tylenol went on to become the No. 1 drugstore product.

Two weeks before the Datril advertising broke, Johnson & Johnson notified Bristol-Myers that it was cutting Tylenol's price to match Datril. Furthermore, Johnson & Johnson also issued credit memorandums to reduce prices on existing stocks in stores.

Hard-headed Bristol-Myers launched their attack anyway. They even advanced the break date of the television commercials so that they ran the day after they were notified of the Tylenol price reduction, apparently figuring it would take days for the price change to filter down to all the nation's 165,000 retail outlets.

All hell broke loose. Johnson & Johnson complained to the networks, the magazines, the Proprietary Association, and the Council of Better Business Bureaus.

The networks asked for copy changes. In the first revision, the "dollar lower" price was changed to "Datril can cost less, a lot less." Another protest from Johnson & Johnson brought deletion of "a lot less." Finally both CBS and NBC refused to run the Datril spots at all, a bitter pill for Bristol-Myers to swallow.

The Johnson & Johnson response worked perfectly. Datril never achieved more than a 1 percent market share.

Tylenol, on the other hand, took off like a rocket. The momentum created by Tylenol's response lifted the brand to the top.

Partly because of the lower price and partly because of the publicity, Tylenol found itself on top of the analgesic market, reaching a high of 37 percent. At one point, Tylenol outsold Anacin, Bufferin, and Bayer combined.

Then tragedy struck in Chicago. Seven people died after taking Tylenol laced with cyanide. But Tylenol came back to regain most of Migraine Mountain, one reason being the fact that there was no strong No. 2 to Tylenol. No alternative for Tylenol users.

If Datril had been less greedy, if Datril had launched a guerrilla war instead of a direct attack . . . but that's another story best left to the chapter on guerrilla warfare.

Be prepared to strike back

What do most companies do when one of their major brands is hit by a price attack?

The classic response is "wait and see." Wait and see if it affects our sales. Wait and see if the competitor can hang in there financially for the long haul. Wait and see if our customers come back after trying the low-priced alternative.

What would your company do if a major competitor suddenly cut its price substantially? Be prepared. The leader should be emotionally ready to strike back.

What would you do? Are you sure?

As the battle for Migraine Mountain proved, there would have been plenty of business for both Johnson & Johnson's high-priced Tylenol and Bristol-Myer's low-priced Datril. But it would not have been good strategy for Johnson & Johnson to share the market.

A live-and-let-live philosophy has no place in warfare. Companies like Johnson & Johnson and Procter & Gamble take no prisoners.

Keeping something in reserve

Another strategy that works well for leaders is to keep "something in reserve."

While an attacker should go all out, it's not always desirable for the leader to spend as much money as possible on marketing operations. Much better to spend only as much as necessary to "keep the competition in line."

Keep the rest as a reserve. Should the competition attack with an unusually attractive offer, you'll have the wherewithal to defend your position.

Anheuser-Busch has used this strategy effectively with their Budweiser beer. They "lay low" in certain markets until Budweiser sales start to falter.

Then they move in with a massive advertising program to get Bud moving again. Called "pulsing," this strategy not only conserves dollars but also provides a reserve for use if and when the competition launches an all-out attack.

"The number of fresh reserves," says Clausewitz, "is always the chief point looked at by both commanders."

What about the feds?

One of the constraints that hold companies in check is the fear of legal reprisals.

And the fear is real, especially for the market leader. Witness the breakup of AT&T. The decade-long antitrust suit against IBM.

A certain amount of legal expense should be considered by defenders as part of their normal cost of doing business. Ralph Nader tells the story of an airline executive who was asked how his company's earnings had fared. "Not bad," the executive replied, "seven times legal fees."

Oddly enough, the defensive strategies suggested here should reduce your legal exposure. Gillette's strategy of attacking itself is probably legally safer than attacking the competition.

Furthermore, the exercise of power vertically to defend a market is also safer than moving horizontally to extend your power into another market. (Many companies have gotten into legal hot water with tie-in sales, joint discounts, and other tactics that exploit their position in one market to try to muscle into another.)

"The mere possession of monopoly power," said Judge Irvin Kaufman in the Berkey-Kodak case, was not necessarily illegal. But it was unlawful for a monopoly to use its power in one area to gain a competitive advantage in another market, "even if there has not been an attempt to monopolize the second market," said the judge.

Marketing peace

The goal of all defensive war, of course, is marketing peace. With the competition reduced to sporadic guerrilla attacks.

You deserve a break today.

When a leader establishes a dominant position in its category, as McDonald's has done in the fast-food category, it should shift its strategy to expanding the market. Who's the enemy of McDonald's? It's the family that eats at home. That's why "You deserve a break today" is such an effective strategy. In 1999, *Advertising Age* voted it the No. 1 jingle of all time. Too bad McDonald's dropped it.

Marketing peace is what Kodak has achieved in photographic film, Campbell's in soup, and IBM in mainframe computers. Each of these companies has a dominant share of its market. So dominant that there are no companies in second place in the mind of the prospect.

Leaders should be wary, however. Wars often occur in pairs, with the second war being started by the loser of the first. World War II was started by Germany, the loser of World War I. The War of 1812 was started by England, the loser of the American Revolutionary War.

Assuming that peace has permanently broken out, leaders can change their strategy. They can shift gears to a generic rather than a brand strategy. Which is why Campbell Soup Company promotes soup rather than Campbell's. "Soup is good food," say the ads—presumably anybody's soup.

And Kodak sells photographic film, not just Kodak film. "Because time goes by," say the television commercials.

When you own the pie, you should try to enlarge the pie rather than try to increase the size of your slice.

Where absolute superiority is not attainable, you must produce a relative one at the decisive point by making skillful use of what you have.   Karl von Clausewitz

8 Principles of offensive warfare

There's no such thing as good marketing strategy in the abstract. Good strategy is bad. And bad strategy is good. It all depends on who is going to use it.

In fact, offensive strategy is exactly the same as defensive strategy except that it's exactly the opposite. The two are so closely related it's hard to separate them.

What's good strategy for a leader is bad strategy for an also-ran, and vice versa. So it's important to constantly ask yourself what position you occupy in the marketplace before you apply strategy.

Leaders should play defensive, not offensive, warfare. Offensive warfare is a game for the No. 2 or No. 3 company in a given field. This is a company strong enough to mount a sustained offensive against the leader.

No one can tell you what "strong enough" means. Like military warfare, marketing warfare is an art, not a science. You have to use your judgment.

In some industries several companies may be strong enough to launch offensive attacks against the leader. In

In ancient times, the Chinese believed that the yin and the yang represented the universe, created in perfect unity. The yin was female; the yang was male. The yin was passive; the yang was active. And so forth. Offensive and defensive warfare are locked together in the same way. What is good strategy for the defender is usually bad strategy for the attacker, and vice versa.

The Curse
of Benjamin Franklin Goodrich:
His Name.

It's one of fate's cruel accidents that our biggest competitor's name turns out to be almost identical to our founder's.

Goodyear. Goodrich.

Awfully confusing. Especially since Goodyear has advertised more than we have.

The fact is, we even think a lot of people who've seen our ads have come away remembering their name. Just because they've seen it so often.

Sure, we could change our name. But we'd rather do

It's hard to become the opposite of the leader when you have a name (BF Goodrich) that's almost the same as the name of the leading brand (Goodyear). Instead of running ads crying about the problem, Goodrich should have changed its name.

other industries, no one is. It would be the height of folly for one of the BUNCH (Burroughs, Univac, NCR, Control Data, and Honeywell) to launch an offensive attack against IBM in mainframe computers.

If your company is strong enough, it should play offensive war. There are three principles to guide you.

Offensive principle No. 1

The main consideration is the strength of the leader's position.

This is exactly the same as the first principle of defensive warfare. But it's much easier for leaders to focus on themselves than it is for a No. 2 or No. 3 companies to focus their attention on the leader.

Most companies are like kids. They want to "do it themselves." Their instant reaction to a marketing problem is to study their navels. To consider their own strengths and weaknesses. The quality of their own product, their own sales force, their own pricing, their own distribution. Which is why most companies end up talking and acting as if they were the leader.

What a No. 2 or No. 3 company should do is to focus on the leader. The leader's product, the leader's sales force, the leader's pricing, the leader's distribution.

No matter how strong a No. 2 company is in a certain category or attribute, it cannot win if this is also where the leader is strong.

What the leader owns is a position in the mind of the prospect. To win the battle of the mind, you must take away the leader's position before you can substitute your own. It's not enough for you to succeed; others must fail. Specifically, the leader.

Several years ago Schenley Industries introduced Ne Plus Ultra, a 12-year-old Scotch whiskey with the highest price on the market. Schenley had high hopes for Ne Plus Ultra; the name is Latin for "nothing finer."

"If people give it a try," said the president of the sales division, "we should have no problem. It's just so very, very smooth."

Trial wasn't the problem. Chivas Regal was. Sales of Ne Plus at the liquor stores registered about D minus. And almost zero at restaurants and bars. (Try saying to your favorite bartender, "I'd like a Ne Plus Ultra.")

The need to focus on the enemy and not yourself was illustrated by a poster widely distributed in World War II. Food conservation was a key concern of the U.S. government at the time so they printed patriotic posters that said "Food Will Win the War."

"I know that food can win the war," said the G.I. looking at his unappetizing K-rations, "but how are we going to get the enemy to eat it?"

Getting the enemy to eat it is the key objective of offensive warfare. The morale factor can be decisive. The emphasis should be on destroying the morale of your opponent.

But it's not easy for a No. 2 company to keep this concept in focus. So most marketing plans call for "increasing our share of the market." In a given field a half dozen companies might develop marketing plans with similar share-increasing objectives. Not to mention the plans of

Traditionally, Scotch is a blended whisky, but Glenlivet and other brands have taken market share from the leading brands by introducing single-malt Scotch whisky. Instead of trying to be a better blended whisky, a better strategy is to be a different whisky. (We misspelled whiskey in the text. The whiskies of Scotland and Canada are always minus an "e." The whiskeys of Ireland and the United States always add an "e.")

new companies that might be invading the territory. No wonder the typical marketing promise is seldom kept.

A much better strategy for No. 2 is to look at the leader and ask yourself, "How do I decrease their share of the market?"

We don't mean undermining leaders by dynamiting their plants or interdicting their rail centers. That's a physical way of looking at marketing warfare.

Never forget that marketing warfare is a mental exercise with the battleground being the human mind. All offensive operations should be directed at that target. Your artillery is nothing but words, pictures, sounds.

Offensive principle No. 2

Find a weakness in the leader's strength and attack at that point.

That's not a misprint. We mean "find a weakness in the leader's strength," not in the leader's weakness.

Sometimes leaders have weak points that are just weak points and not an inherent part of their strength. They may have overlooked the point, considered it unimportant, or forgotten about it.

The high price of Tylenol ($2.85 for 100 tablets) was not an inherent weakness in the Johnson & Johnson brand. One hundred 325-mg Tylenol tablets contain about 5 cents' worth of acetaminophen. Johnson & Johnson could easily reduce Tylenol's price, as they demonstrated with devastating results to Datril.

Nor is high price an inherent weakness in IBM computers. Because of the scale of its production, IBM has

Mercedes-Benz made big, comfortable, prestigious vehicles, so BMW attacked with smaller, more nimble machines. "The ultimate driving machine" is how BMW expressed its position. Today, BMW outsells Mercedes in the U.S. market and in most countries of the world. We advise clients to "become the opposite of the leader," a variation on offensive principle No. 2: "Find a weakness in the leader's strength."

the lowest manufacturing cost in the industry. It's always dangerous to attack IBM on price because they have the financial ability to make money at almost any price, no matter how low.

But there is another kind of weakness, a weakness that grows out of strength. As the Avis ads used to say, "Rent from Avis. The line at our counter is shorter."

Short of shooting some of its customers, its hard to see how Hertz can counter this strategy. This is a weakness inherent in Hertz's position as the largest rent-a-car company, as it is for most leaders.

The only success American Motors enjoyed in recent years was with its Buyer's Protection Plan, which was an attack against the poor service reputation of most General Motors dealers. Like Hertz, GM is the victim of its own success. The more cars a dealer sells in its showroom up front, the more problems the dealer creates for the service area in the back.

Price isn't always something for an attacker to avoid. When it's inherent in a strength, price can be used very effectively. An example involves the Radio Advertising Bureau, a group organized to promote the merits of radio advertising.

Who is the leader in media advertising? Television is. TV not only sells $18 billion worth of advertising time a year—it also owns the minds of most buyers.

Where is television strong? Part of the mystique of TV is its reach. One show, like the Super Bowl, can reach 60 percent of the homes in America.

Where is television weak? Well, reaching all those homes is expensive. One minute of commercial time on

Listerine is the bad-tasting mouthwash and used to brag about it: "The taste you hate. Twice a day." Scope became a strong No. 2 brand by being the opposite: a good-tasting mouthwash.

the Super Bowl program is currently priced at over $1 million. And the price keeps going up.

World War II cost the U.S. government $9000 a minute. The Vietnam war cost $22,000 a minute. And now it will cost you $1,000,000 a minute for advertising on the Super Bowl. War is expensive, but marketing is no slouch either.

"How do you spell 'relief' from the pain of high TV costs?" asks the headline of a Radio Advertising Bureau advertisement. And the answer is R-A-D-I-O.

Radio is inexpensive, as everyone knows. But to drive home this idea, the low price of radio needs to be tied into the high cost of television.

Offensive principle No. 3

Launch the attack on as narrow a front as possible.

Preferably with a single product. The "full line" is a luxury only leaders can afford. Offensive warfare should be waged with narrow lines, as close to single products as possible.

This is an area where marketing people have a lot to learn from the military. In World War II, offensive attacks were usually launched on a very narrow front. Sometimes down a single highway. Only when a breakthrough was achieved did the attacking forces expand laterally to occupy territory.

When you attack on a narrow front, you're putting the principle of force to work for you. You are massing your forces to achieve a local superiority. "Where absolute superiority is not attainable," says Clausewitz, "you must

Concentrated attacks on a narrow front.

Spreading your forces on a wide front.

You would think that a concentrated attack on a narrow front would obviously be better than spreading your forces over a wide front. But a lot of management people think otherwise. Consider Dell vs. Hewlett-Packard. Dell has a narrow line of products sold direct. Hewlett-Packard has a wide range of products sold in a number of different channels. Which company has the better strategy? Dell, of course.

produce a relative one at the decisive point by making skillful use of what you have."

The marketing army that tries to gain as much territory as fast as possible by attacking all at once on a wide front with a broad line of products will surely lose in the long run all the territory it has gained. And a lot more, too.

Yet that's exactly what many No. 2 or No. 3 companies try to do. "We didn't have the luxury of passing up any automobile market in the United States," said Chrysler President Lynn Townsend—an attitude that contributed to Chrysler's problems in the past.

And the head of American Motors publicly complains that AMC participates in only 25 percent of the market. Presumably what comes next is broadening of the AMC product line and further weakening of its sales.

The odds favor the defender

It's not every day that David goes out and slays Goliath. Offensive warfare is not an easy task.

The second principle of Clausewitz says that the odds favor the defender. Statistics show that most attacks are going to fail. In a survey of 600 companies over a 2-year period, only 20 percent enjoyed market share gains of 2 percent or more. In other words, four out of five companies made negligible gains or actually lost ground.

When you look at the age of the companies, you can see how market shares get frozen into fixed positions over time, the way World War I degenerated into trench warfare where gains were registered in yards instead of miles.

Linux became a big brand by being the opposite of Microsoft Windows. Windows cost money; Linux was free. Windows was proprietary; Linux was open-source software. And so forth.

Of those companies that were 5 years old or younger, 40 percent increased market share. Of those companies that were 20 years old or older, only 17 percent increased market share.

Clearly offensive warfare is a game for only the most determined and skillful marketing people. But you can greatly increase your chances of success by careful analysis of the leader's strength.

The weakness in strength

There's weakness in strength, if you can find it. Achilles had a heel which led to his downfall.

As a company increases its share of the market beyond a certain point, it becomes weaker, not stronger. These 60, 70, 80 percent market share brands look exceedingly strong; yet they are sometimes vulnerable . . . if you can find the weakness inherent in their strength.

Take amateur color photographic film. This is a billion dollar market in America and Kodak has an 85 percent market share. (Kodak's pretax profit margins are reported to be upward of 50 percent.)

Clearly this is a yellow monster with considerable clout. To attack such a beast successfully takes a well-thought-out strategy.

Forget price. With its high profit margins, Kodak could cut its prices in half and still make money. Furthermore, the film price is the smaller half of the package. Most amateur photographers use color print film which must be developed and printed, a process which costs more than the film itself.

Every strength has a weakness. As Yogi Berra once said, "Nobody goes there anymore. It was getting too popular."

Forget quality. Most photographers couldn't tell the difference. Even if it were possible to produce a color film with a demonstrable difference in quality, the world's largest maker of color film (Kodak) could be expected to match it in short order.

Forget finding a weakness that's just a weakness. Turn the problem around and look at Kodak's strengths. Where is Kodak strong in photographic film?

The answer is everywhere. The ubiquitousness of that little yellow box is one of Kodak's major strengths.

No matter where you are, you can count on being able to pick up a box of Kodak film. At almost every super-market, drugstore, newspaper stand, or candy store in the country. There are almost 200,000 Kodak film outlets in America alone. And the instruction sheet is printed in eight languages.

Universal availability is an enormous benefit to the film user. No matter where you are in the world, you can always buy a box of Kodak film. Since film users like to standardize on one brand, Kodak is the obvious choice.

Where is the weakness inherent in that strength? If you look at the box, you'll see a "process before" date. Kodak makes photographic film like Brie makes cheese and Chiquita makes bananas. Kodak makes it "green" and it ripens on the shelf. If the film gets overripe, the prints are off-color, often pinkish, and always a big disappointment.

Kodak pays for its ubiquitousness by having to put up with the aging process that takes place at room temperature.

Photographic film is produced the way bananas are picked. It is manufactured "green," and it ripens in the distribution channel.

Photographic film.

TRUCOLOR

Keep refrigerated.

To compete with Kodak, we suggested that 3M introduce a photographic film that was ready to be used as it came off the production line—hence the name Trucolor.

Like bananas, color film can be manufactured "ripe." But unlike bananas, color film will stay that way if kept refrigerated. (Which is why Kodak professional film is manufactured ripe and kept refrigerated until it's sold.)

So our offensive strategy for a Kodak competitor is to launch the world's first refrigerated color film for the amateur market. Then give it a name like "Trucolor" to communicate the idea that the film hasn't deteriorated on the shelf before you bought it.

Of course, you couldn't sell Trucolor film in most of Kodak's 200,000 outlets because many of them don't have refrigeration equipment. That's all right. Kodak has those outlets locked up anyway. They don't need another brand.

Where you could sell Trucolor film is in the freezer section of the supermarket. Sell it in six-packs and tell the customer to keep the film in the refrigerator until ready to use.

Who knows, someday there might be a film container in your Frigidaire in addition to the butter container.

But first someone must see the potential of the Trucolor concept which has already been turned down cold by 3M, America's second largest film manufacturer. A distant second, to be sure.

The same kind of thinking can be used against any big, ubiquitous brand. How would you go against Campbell's soup, for example? Forget taste, forget price. As a matter of fact, forget everything that's inside the can and concentrate on the can itself. That's where Campbell is vulnerable.

Cans rust. But Campbell has hundreds of millions of dollars worth of can-making equipment that they can't walk away from very easily. But such limitations wouldn't affect a new competitor who could try plastic, glass, or aseptic packaging. Then play "kick the can" with Campbell's.

Don't expect any company to pick up on these concepts soon. Good offensive ideas are extremely difficult to sell because they are negative in nature. They go against the "positive thinking" grain of most management people.

How would you compete with market leader Campbell's soup? Package your soup in glass or plastic and then badmouth the cans. Some soup producers do that with one hand tied behind their backs. They emphasize the positive (glass), but they don't emphasize the negative (cans can rust).

The benefits of being narrow-minded

Another idea that was hard to sell was Federal Express. Fred Smith's professor at Yale gave him a C when he turned in an economics paper describing the concept.

But that didn't deter Mr. Smith. A decade later, Federal Express was a profitable competitor in the package express business . . . after $80 million worth of venture capital was poured into the company.

Federal had a lot going for it. The system was designed to move only parcels and envelopes, nothing over 70 pounds. It was the first airline delivery service to operate exclusively through a hub-and-spokes pattern. Nothing traveled point to point, but rather all packages came to a central hub in Memphis to be sorted and rerouted via an outbound flight.

The hub-and-spokes concept was a technological breakthrough, not unlike the English longbow used at Crecy in 1346.

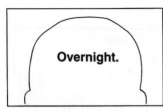

Overnight.

To test your marketing strategy, ask yourself, "What word do we want to own in the mind?" Federal Express decided to try to own the word *overnight,* and in the process the company became a phenomenal success. So what word is the company trying to own today? We'll bet that most people don't know the theme, "Relax, it's FedEx," in spite of the fact that the company is spending a fortune on advertising ($88.5 million in a recent year). What it should do is go back to the original: "When it absolutely, positively has to be there overnight." The implication is if FedEx can do a great job on overnight service, it can probably do a great job on two- and three-day service, too.

In spite of its Memphis longbow, Federal wasn't an overnight success. At first Federal tried to compete with air freight forwarders like Emery and Airborne with three classes of services: Priorities One, Two, and Three (for overnight, 2-day, and 3-day deliveries). Basically the Federal Express advertising said, "We've got our own planes and trucks, so we're more reliable and less expensive."

It was a mistake. Losses the first 2 years were $29 million. The full line is a luxury for the leader. Offensive principle No. 3 says *launch the attack on as narrow a front as possible.*

Then Federal reorganized and changed its marketing strategy. The focus would be on Priority One. "When it absolutely, positively has to be there overnight," said the massive television advertising which was a cornerstone of the new strategy.

Over the years the results of this narrow-minded strategy have been spectacular. Today Federal Express dominates the small-package air-express market. Operating revenues are over $1 billion a year, as much as Emery and Airborne combined.

The disadvantages of being broad-minded

One company that learned to appreciate the need to attack with a single product is Management Science America, the largest independent supplier of mainframe computer software. MSA tried to get into the personal computer software business with the purchase of Peachtree Software.

But MSA proceeded to run Peachtree as if it were the leader instead of an also-ran. In a typical move Peachtree introduced 25 different software products in a campaign called "The Big Bang." MSA's chairman boasted that by promoting the quality of a family of microcomputer programs, Peachtree would move ahead of such companies as Lotus Development that depended heavily on a single hit like "1-2-3."

The Peachtree Big Bang was launched with a massive marketing campaign, including a heavy advertising program. Yet less than 2 years later, MSA declared its venture into the personal software business a failure and announced that it would sell or spin off its Peachtree operation.

To make matters worse, while MSA was preoccupied with Peachtree, it was losing ground in its mainframe software business. Currently, Cullinet Software is growing at a faster pace than MSA and breathing down its neck.

In his book *The World on Time*, James C. Wetherbe outlines the 11 management principles that made FedEx an overnight sensation. Which management principle do you suppose covers the concept of narrowing the focus to "overnight" deliveries? That's right. It's totally ignored.

Attacking a monopoly

Monopolies look especially strong. But even a company with almost 100 percent of a market can be successfully attacked—if you can find a weakness inherent in strength.

Take *The Wall Street Journal,* with a circulation over 2 million. Not only is the *Journal* the largest newspaper in America, but it also carries more advertising than any other print medium. A tempting target you might say. But no one is taking a shot at it.

Let us take a verbal shot at it. How did *The Wall Street Journal* get to be so big?

THE WALL STREET JOURNAL.

MARKETPLACE

MONEY & INVESTING

The Wall Street Journal has three regular sections. Marketplace is all business. Money & Investing is all financial. And the front section is half and half. A good offensive strategy is to focus on one segment of a leader's position. The business half of the *Journal* would have been our choice.

Great writers, great editorials, you might say. So you might consider attacking the *Journal* with a better editorial product. But that's not good military thinking. A good general tries to avoid depending on quality of personnel for his margin of victory. A good general wants relative superiority at the decisive point.

A good marketing general would not try to outwrite the *Journal.*

How did the *Journal* get so big? If you look at the publication closely, you find it's actually two newspapers in one: a business paper covering business news—new products, new plants, new marketing campaigns, etc.—and a financial newspaper covering stocks, bonds, corporate earnings, etc.

To prove that point, we actually took one copy of the *Journal* and cut it up, putting business news and advertisements in one pile and financial news and advertisements in another. The two piles were approximately the same height.

Which side should you attack? The name "Wall Street" positions the *Journal* as a financial paper. So the business side would be a better point of attack.

"Business Times, the daily business newspaper," would be a good name and position. Business readers wouldn't have to wade through such financial news as the City of Chattanooga's new 10⅞% municipal bonds. And the business advertiser wouldn't have to pay for all that wasted circulation. (At $75,355.68 a page, the cost of running an advertising program in the *Journal* can mount up in a hurry.)

The *Business Times* strategy evolves directly from the three principles of offensive warfare.

Principle No. 1: *The main consideration is the strength of the leader's position.* In other words, focus on the *Journal's* position, not your own.

Principle No. 2: *Find a weakness in the leader's strength and attack at that point.* Like most monopolies, the *Journal* has become all things to all people. That's a strength that can become a weakness.

Principle No. 3: *Launch the attack on as narrow a front as possible.* A daily business newspaper would attack the *Journal* at half of its front.

Wouldn't it take $50 to $100 million to launch a *Business Times?* Yes, it would. But that's less than Gannett is spending to get *USA Today* off the ground, a venture with much less chance of success.

USA Today is a flanking move against an uncertain market. *Business Times* would be against a market that represents a quarter of a billion in advertising revenue alone.

You can afford to spend more on an offensive attack because you know the market is there. A flanking attack is always a speculative venture.

Pursuit is a second act of the victory, in many cases more important than the first.   Karl von Clausewitz

9 Principles of flanking warfare

For most marketing managers, offensive and defensive are natural strategies. The leader defends, everyone else attacks. So what else is new?

Flanking. For most managers, flanking warfare may seem like a military concept with no marketing applications. Not so. Flanking is the most innovative way to fight a marketing war.

Most military commanders devote much of their planning time searching for ways to launch flanking attacks. America's last significant land victory was a flanking attack: MacArthur's landings at Inchon in 1950. Such attacks are not always successful, a notable example being the failure at Anzio 6 years earlier.

In both a marketing and a military sense, a flanking operation is a bold move. A big gamble with big stakes. One that requires detailed planning on an hour-by-hour, day-to-day basis.

You might say a general accepts offensive and defensive assignments as a normal part of the job, but lives for

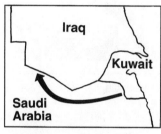

At the start of the first Iraqi war, the U.S. Army and its allies were encamped in Kuwait and eastern Saudi Arabia. Naturally, the Iraqis assumed that the invasion would come from the east. So General H. Norman Schwarzkopf shifted 150,000 Allied forces 100 miles west and launched his major attack from the south, taking the enemy by surprise. After 100 hours, the Iraqi defense collapsed and the United States declared the war over.

the day he is chosen to lead a flanking attack. It's the best hope for achieving a big, spectacular victory.

More than any other form of warfare, flanking requires a knowledge of the principles involved and an ability to visualize how the battle will unfold after the attack is launched. These are much the same skills a good chess player develops.

Flanking principle No. 1

Why would you attack a leader head-on when you can go around him? This simple analogy can be a powerful marketing tool.

A good flanking move must be made into an uncontested area.

You don't drop your paratroops on top of the enemy's machine-gun positions, and you don't launch a flanking product into the teeth of an established product.

A flanking move does not necessarily require a new product unlike anything now on the market. But there must be some element of newness or exclusivity. The prospect must put you into a new category.

Digital Equipment flanked IBM with a small computer which customers put into a new category called "minicomputers"—as opposed to IBM's mainframe computers.

It might not be obvious, but the success of a flanking attack often hinges on your ability to create and maintain a separate category. This is not always easy, especially since the defender can be expected to try to blunt the attack by denying the existence of the new category.

Traditional marketing theory might call this approach *segmentation,* the search for segments or niches. This is an important qualification. To launch a true flanking attack, you must be the first to occupy the segment. Otherwise, it's just an offensive attack against a defended position.

The two are quite different. Undefended, a hill or segment of a market could be taken by a squad. Defended, the same hill might require the best efforts of an entire division to capture.

Flanking skill requires exceptional foresight. The reason is that in a true flanking attack, there is no established market for the new product or service.

That makes it tough on the B-school types who have nothing to feed into their computers. When Miller flanked the industry with Lite, what was the market for light beer? Zip, of course.

Today Americans drink 35 million barrels of the stuff, the majority of which has been brewed by Miller.

Mercedes-Benz flanked Cadillac by selling more expensive cars. But Mercedes continues to undermine its high-end position by selling cheaper versions of its luxury cars, such as its A-class and C-class vehicles.

It's difficult for a traditional marketer to market a product with no market. But that's exactly what you have to try to do if you want to launch a successful flanking attack.

Where will the business come from if there is no market to start with? From the competitors whose shoulders you are flanking. This unraveling of the enemy's strength is the essence of a successful flanking maneuver. It can create enormous momentum which can be extremely difficult for the competitor to stop.

When Mercedes-Benz flanked Cadillac at the high end of the automotive market, it was precisely the same Cadillac buyers who fueled the movement to Mercedes. After all, the Cadillac buyer was used to "buying the best." Only the introduction of the higher-priced Seville helped Cadillac recover somewhat.

Flanking principle No. 2

Tactical surprise ought to be an important element of the plan.

By its nature, a flanking attack is a surprise attack. In this respect, it's different from offensive or defensive warfare where the nature and direction of attacks are pretty much expected. (If Ford is going to attack General Motors, they have to attack somewhere between Chevrolet and Cadillac.)

But flanking is different. The most successful flanking moves are the ones that are totally unexpected. The greater the surprise, the longer it will take the leader to react and try to cover.

Surprise also tends to demoralize the competition. Their sales force is temporarily tongue-tied. They often don't know what to say until they get directions from headquarters.

Unfortunately, great flanking moves are often undermined by test-marketing or too much research, which exposes the strategy to the competition.

The classic example is Datril, which never had a chance because their test-marketing alerted the folks at Johnson & Johnson to the potential danger.

Test-marketing a proposed flanking attack is a catch-22 proposition. If it fails, it fails. If it succeeds, it alerts the leader to take the steps necessary to ensure failure when the test-marketing is expanded to a regional or national basis.

What if the leader is foolish enough to ignore your successful market test? Then, of course, you might be able to launch the product or service on a national basis and

Apple's iPod, the first hard-drive MP3 player, has become the must-have product for the younger generation. Apple's chairman, Steve Jobs, is famous for keeping new products under wraps until his company is ready to launch them.

have a big winner. In other words, you keep your fingers crossed and hope the competition won't notice what you're doing.

You might get lucky. On the other hand, taking a chance like this violates a cardinal principle of military planning: Base your strategy on what your enemy is able to do, not just on what he is likely to do.

Flanking principle No. 3

The pursuit is just as critical as the attack itself.

This is the pour-it-on principle. "Without pursuit," says Clausewitz, "no victory can have a great effect."

Too many companies, however, quit after they're ahead. They achieve their initial marketing targets and then they move resources on to other endeavors.

That's a mistake, especially in a flanking move. Ancient military maxim: Reinforce success, abandon failure.

Let's say a company has five products, three winners and two losers. Who do you think gets the time and attention of top management? That's right, the losers.

It should be just the opposite. Shoot the losers and send their petrol rations to the tank commanders who are making the most progress.

It's exactly the same as that classic principle for making money in the stock market. Cut your losses and let your winners ride.

Yet for reasons that are more emotional than economic, many companies can't deal with success. They tend to ignore the future and spend all their marketing money trying to recover from strategic mistakes made in the past.

When you have a flanking product that starts to become successful, you ought to really pour it on. Your objective ought to be to win and win big.

Too often, the emphasis inside a marketing operation is to protect the company from a loser. Much time and effort is spent protecting old products and old markets. Little consideration is given to reinforcing success.

The best time to build a strong position is in the beginning, when the product is new and exciting and the competion is scarce or running scared. This is a luxury you seldom enjoy for long.

The big flanking successes of recent years (Fantastik spray cleaner, Close-Up toothpaste, Lite beer) all spent heavily "up front"—before they were successful, not after.

Success breeds success. It's important to use your marketing weight to get your new product off the ground in a hurry, *before* the leader can cover and you get overwhelmed by a parade of me-too products.

What if you don't have the resources to follow up the launch of a successful flanking attack? That's a real possibility in many fields—automobiles, beer, computers, to name three that quickly come to mind.

Perhaps you shouldn't have launched a flanking attack in the first place. Perhaps you should have waged guerrilla warfare.

Marketing history is filled with stories of flanking attacks that were initially successful, yet ultimately went nowhere because of lack of resources to follow through.

The full name of the product was the MITS Altair 8800. Why is it that the first brand in a new category is usually given a long and complicated name? The first cell phone was the Motorola DynaTAC 8000X. The first computer was the ENIAC, an acronym for electronic numerical integrator and computer. The winners are usually the brands with the simpler and shorter names— Apple and Nokia, for example.

Remember the Altair? Launched in 1975 by a company called MITS, the Altair was the world's first personal computer. But the company didn't have the resources to keep up, so MITS was sold to a conglomerate in 1977 where it withered and died 2 years later. From pioneer to pasture in just 4 years. (Ed Roberts, the founder of MITS, took his Altair profits and bought a Georgia farm.)

In many ways Altair was a victim of its own success. The monster market it created eventually attracted bigger players with more resources.

Most companies will never have the opportunity to launch a personal computer. Most companies will have to settle for introducing more mundane products. How do you spot flanking opportunities in your product category? Let's review some typical flanking moves.

Flanking with low price

The most obvious form of flanking is low price. The advantage of this approach is that the market is there. After all, everyone presumably wants to save money. Yet it's tough to make money by cutting prices.

You can make a lot of money with a low-price flanking move. John Osher and three other Cleveland-area entrepreneurs developed the first battery-operated toothbrush that could be sold for $5.00. Called SpinBrush, the product was introduced in 1998. Two years later, SpinBrush was sold to Procter & Gamble for $475 million, a big payout for an investment that totaled $1.5 million.

The trick is to cut costs in areas where customers won't notice or don't care; the no-frills approach.

Fifteen years ago, Days Inns flanked Holiday Inns at the low end of the motel market. Today Days Inns is the eighth-largest lodging chain in America and one of the most profitable.

Budget flanked Hertz and Avis at the low end of the rent-a-car market. Today Budget is fighting it out with National for third place in the market. Note, however, the

Another example of a high-price flanking move is Absolut vodka. Priced 50 percent higher than the leading brand (Smirnoff), Absolut has become an enormous success. Was the brilliant Absolut advertising a critical element? Sure, but the advertising wouldn't have worked nearly as well without the higher price. What Absolut did to Smirnoff, Grey Goose did to Absolut, flanking the brand with an even higher price. Seven years after its introduction, Grey Goose was sold to Bacardi Ltd. for the astounding price of $2 billion, the largest in liquor history for a single brand.

importance of the pour-it-on principle. Budget was first and expanded at a furious pace. Budget now has more than 1200 locations in 37 countries around the world. This fast-moving pursuit is keeping Budget well ahead of low-priced copycat competitors like Dollar, Thrifty, and Econo-Car.

And in 1975 a company called Savin caught Xerox off guard with small, inexpensive copiers made by Ricoh in Japan. Savin was soon boasting in its advertisements that it was placing more copiers in America than Xerox and IBM combined.

In the airline industry, PEOPLExpress is flying high with a classic low-price, no-frills strategy.

Flanking with high price

Psychologist Robert B. Cialdini tells the story of a jewelry store in Arizona that couldn't sell an allotment of turquoise pieces. Just before leaving on a trip, the owner scribbled a note to her head salesperson—"Everything in this case, price × 1/2,"—hoping to get rid of the jewelry, even at a loss. When she returned a few days later, every article was gone. But because the salesperson had read the 1/2 in the scrawled message as a 2, the entire batch had been sold at twice the original price, not half.

For many products, high price is a benefit. The price adds credibility to the product. Joy, for example, is advertised as the "costliest perfume in the world." With Joy, the price is the benefit.

There are many opportunities for high-price flanking moves. Take popcorn. In 1975 Hunt-Wesson spent $6 million to advertise Orville Redenbacher's Gourmet Popping Corn. (The entire popcorn category that year generated only $85 million in sales.)

Priced 2½ times higher than the leading brand, Orville Redenbacher took off. Four years later it was the nation's No. 1 brand of popcorn, in spite of the fact that the label says "World's most expensive popping corn."

Even such bastions of low price as the supermarket industry are having a high-price fling. Gourmet supermarkets selling such deluxe items as lobsters, truffles, and caviar, as well as the usual fare of dog food and detergents, are starting to open. On the East coast of America, Grand Union has opened 34 gourmet supermarkets called The Food Emporium. In Minneapolis, Byerly's is a six-store minichain with carpeted aisles and crystal chandeliers. Byerly's is America's first designer supermarket.

Another classic high-price flank is Haagen-Dazs, the super-premium ice cream.

Haagen-Dazs was the first high-butterfat ice cream. Today it outsells all other super premiums combined.

There's hardly a category where someone has not established a successful high-price flank. From automobiles (Mercedes) to banking (Morgan Guaranty) to beer (Michelob), from the Concorde airplane to the Concord watch, almost any product or service represents a golden opportunity to strike at the high end.

There are two good reasons why high price represents more of a marketing opportunity than low price. One is the tendency of the prospect to equate quality with price. "You get what you pay for." The other is the potential for higher profit margins with a higher price. The higher mar-

The fastest-growing supermarket chain in America is Whole Foods Market. Not only does Whole Foods have higher prices. It also focuses on organic foods.

Lexus wasn't the first high-priced Japanese car. Acura was. But Lexus won the marketing battle by selling expensive six- and eight-cylinder cars exclusively. Acura also sold relatively inexpensive four-cylinder cars, thereby muddying its brand.

gins allow you to finance the critical "pursuit" stage of a flanking attack.

Flanking with small size

A typical example of flanking with small size is Sony. Using integrated circuits, Sony pioneered a host of innovative miniaturized products, including Tummy Television, Walkman, and Watchman.

But the classic flanking attack of all time has to be the Beetle. The automotive industry has never been the same since Volkswagen outflanked General Motors.

General Motors made big cars; Volkswagen made small cars.

General Motors had the engines in the front; Volkswagen had the engines in the rear.

General Motors made good-looking cars; the Beetle was an ugly car.

"Think small," said the Volkswagen ad as the company led the assault against Fortress Detroit. A classic flanking attack.

But at the first opportunity, Volkswagen started to think big. In rapid succession, Volkswagen introduced the eight-passenger Wagon, the four-door 411 and the 412 sedans, the sporty Dasher, and the Jeep-type vehicle which Volkswagen called the "Thing."

"Different Volks for different folks," said the ads in an attempt to become all things to all people.

What does Clausewitz say about this strategy? *"Seine Kräfte in einem überwiegenden Masse vereinigt halten. Die*

The classic line extension advertisement. Trying to be all things to all people is the biggest mistake a company can make.

Grundidee, überall zuerst und nach Möglichkeit gesucht werden."

Clausewitz is one of theirs. Volkswagen management could have read his words of wisdom in the original German.

Most of us had to wait for the translation. "Keep the forces concentrated in an overpowering mass. The fundamental idea. Always to be aimed at before all and as far as possible." This is probably the single most-quoted concept of Clausewitz in the military academies of the world and it bears repeating.

From a marketing point of view, Volkswagen spread its forces thin by trying to cover too many different products under one name. A dangerously weak formation.

What happened next could have easily been predicted. It was "Tora, Tora, Tora"—or rather Toyota, Datsun, Honda—as the Japanese poured through the thin Volkswagen line.

At one point in time, Volkswagen had 67 percent of the imported car market in America. That was the year they sold 19 times as many cars as the No. 2 importer. Currently, Volkswagen has less than 7 percent of the import market.

The company has come full circle. Thinking small made Volkswagen big. Thinking big made Volkswagen small again.

Ten years ago Volkswagen reintroduced the Beetle in the U.S. market. The Beetle 2.0 was an immediate success. People looked at the small, ugly, reliable car and thought, "Now, that's a Volkswagen." Volkswagen hit bottom in 1995, when its share of the imported car market dropped to 4 percent. Today, thanks in part to the new Beetle, it is 6 percent.

Flanking with large size

Another flanking pioneer is Howard Head, the founder of Head Ski Company. After selling his ski company, Mr.

Head turned his attention to tennis and started to think big.

In 1976 Head's company, Prince Manufacturing, introduced the oversized tennis racquet. In spite of the fact that scoffers called it "the cheater's" racquet, the new Prince product came to dominate the quality racquet market. By 1984 it had captured a leading 30 percent share.

But that wasn't enough for Prince—or rather Chesebrough-Pond's, who had recently bought the company. So Prince introduced a line of midsize tennis racquets, 25 percent smaller than the original Prince.

So you can expect to see the history repeat itself. Prince got big by thinking big. Prince is now determined to think small and in the process get small.

In the words of one tennis shop owner, "They're not dancing with the person who brung 'em to the ball."

Flanking with distribution

Another powerful strategy is flanking the competition's distribution. You can sometimes flank strongly entrenched competitors by opening up a new distribution channel.

Watches used to be sold almost exclusively in jewelry and department stores until Timex flanked the established brands by using drugstores.

Avon was the first company to use door-to-door selling of cosmetics, a move that flanked several established forms of distribution. (Avon was following the path blazed by Fuller Brush and others.)

Perhaps the most striking distribution flanking move was by Hanes Corportion. In the early seventies, Hanes scored with L'eggs, an inexpensive pantyhose sold on free-standing racks in food and drugstore outlets. With innovative packaging and a strong advertising campaign, L'eggs in 5 years captured 13 percent of the entire pantyhose market.

A distribution flank can be one of the most effective flanking moves you can make. Today, L'eggs is the No. 1 pantyhose brand in America. (Dell is another good example of a distribution flank.)

Flanking with product form

The toothpaste category hasn't been the same since Procter & Gamble's Crest won the American Dental Association's seal of approval and rocketed into first place. But several toothpaste brands since then have made progress with flanking moves based on product form.

The first was from Lever in the early seventies, a time when most toothpastes were exactly that, pastes. But Lever reasoned that a clear mouthwash-looking product would promise the consumer fresher breath. But it would also need abrasives if the product was going to whiten your teeth.

Two Lever scientists found silica abrasives, never before used in toothpaste, which made a translucent gel formulation possible. The result was Close-Up, a clear red gel which rapidly moved into third place in toothpaste sales.

You might think the gel formula was the result of a serendipitous discovery in the laboratory, and you'd be wrong. The concept of Close-Up, a clear red gel combining a tooth whitener and a mouthwash, was a marketing strategy. The scientists were looking for compounds to make the concept work. Therein lie the tactical benefits of good strategic thinking. If you know what it is you're looking for, you can recognize it a lot easier when you find it.

Lever's next move was also brilliant. They decided to add a fluoride to Close-Up. Objective: children in the cavity years between the ages of 6 and 12.

But they didn't do what Volkswagen did. No line extensions for Lever. No Close-Up with Fluoride. They introduced a brand-new brand called Aim.

The great toothpaste wars have been won and lost in the mouth. The votes of the kids often decide the brand for the family. And kids vote sweet.

Aim was a sweet-tasting gel with fluoride, and like Close-Up it also took off. Together the two brands have 20 percent or so of the market.

But a company called Beecham proved there was more than one way to play the breath-freshening plus cavity-fighting game. Several years after Aim's spectacular rise, Beecham introduced Aqua-fresh, the double-protection toothpaste. The difference was visible. Aqua-fresh was a combination of a white paste (fights cavities) plus a blue gel (freshens breath).

The visible difference plus the double-protection theme vaulted Aqua-fresh into third place, ahead of both Aim and Close-Up.

As a concept, flanking with a different form is not limited to toothpaste. Almost any product lends itself to this technique.

Take bar soap, for example. One of the oldest product categories in marketing, bar soap has survived a range of additives starting with the air that allows Ivory to float.

Aquafresh continues to do well in a tough competitive category dominated by two powerhouse brands, Colgate and Crest. A key factor is the visual difference in the Aquafresh product. Whenever possible, companies should try to build visual differences into their brands (the band of a Rolex watch, the polo player on a Ralph Lauren shirt, the slice of lime on a bottle of Corona, the blue color of a Tiffany's package, and so on).

Over the years, there has been perfume (Camay) and deodorants (Dial) as well as moisturizing cream (Dove). The latest form is Softsoap, the original liquid soap.

Softsoap demonstrates the importance of being first. At one point, there were 50 liquid soaps on the market. Today most of these copycats are gone, leaving Softsoap in the No. 1 position.

Flanking with fewer calories

In an era when many people are hit by fitness fever, Stouffer introduced "Lean Cuisine," a single-serving frozen entree with less than 300 calories.

People are jogging. Health clubs are springing up all over the place. No wonder Lean Cuisine was an instant success. In less than a year, Lean Cuisine captured 10 percent of the frozen-entree market.

In classic military style, Stouffer introduced the product with a major push. No tiptoeing into the market. No extensive test-marketing.

The Lean Cuisine advertising launch was also big and bold. In the first year Lean Cuisine accounted for one-third of all frozen-entree advertising.

Also in classic pursuit style, Stouffer continues to keep the Lean Cuisine pressure on. As the brand grows, it dominates the market, effectively blocking competitors.

Factors in successful flanking

Flanking is not for the timid or cautious. It's a gamble with the possibility of a big payoff or a big loss. Further-

Stouffer's Light

Stouffer's Light was the original name of the Lean Cuisine brand, but the name tested poorly. In spite of the fact that almost all truly successful products have new names (Red Bull, Starbucks, Google, Amazon, eBay, Lexus, and so on), most companies cling stubbornly to a line extension strategy when it comes to picking names for new products.

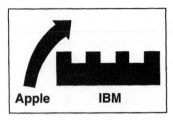

Apple Computer successfully flanked IBM at the low end to dominate the 8-bit home computer market for decades.

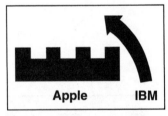

IBM returned the favor by flanking the 8-bit Apple computer at the high end with its 16-bit PC. This was perhaps the most important product introduction of the twentieth century, marred only by the poor choice of name. IBM should have used a different brand name. (Would Toyota have been as successful at the high end if the product had been called Toyota Supreme instead of Lexus? Silly question.)

more, a flanking attack requires vision and foresight. What's the market for an oversize tennis racquet? Before Prince made its move, there was no market at all.

Research-minded marketing managers often find the flanking concept particularly difficult. They tend to substitute research for foresight.

"Would you buy an oversize racquet, Mr. McEnroe?" That's a question that shouldn't be asked of anybody.

Prospects cannot know what they are likely to buy in the future if their choices are going to change drastically. A good flanking move is one that substantially affects the available choices.

"Would you buy a personal computer for $2000?" Ten years ago, most people would have said no. Today many of those same people are walking out of ComputerLand with Apples and IBM PCs.

A flanker often needs the cooperation of the industry leader to achieve success. It was a misreading of the personal computer market potential on the part of IBM that allowed Apple to get off to a running start. IBM's gift to Apple was 4 years of time. Suppose you're considering a flanking move. How much time can you count on?

One way to get a feel for the situation is to read the trade press. Leaders are usually remarkably open with their thoughts about the future. If they have taken a public position against a certain development, you can usually count on additional time. Before they can copy you, they have to "swallow their egos." That can take a while.

Another factor is production lead time. Volkswagen could count on many years before General Motors could put a small car in the marketplace. Even an annual model change in the automobile industry takes 3 years from design to production. A totally new type of car like a sub-compact takes a lot longer. The first Volkswagen hit the New Jersey beach in 1949. It wasn't until 1959 that General Motors rolled out the first Corvair.

By then the Germans had been joined by the Japanese and the small-car invasion was in high gear.

Defending generals realize that the best place to blunt an invasion is on the beaches where the enemy has the sea to their backs. So it is with marketing.

Unfortunately for General Motors and the rest of the American auto industry, when they got around to moving against the small cars, the imports had long since driven from the beaches to the cities and towns.

Another classic flanking success was the Chrysler minivan. So important was the minivan to the company's success that Chrysler touted itself in advertisements as "the minivan company."

The enemy advances, we retreat. The enemy camps, we harass. The enemy tires, we attack. The enemy retreats, we pursue.

Mao Tse-Tung

10 Principles of guerrilla warfare

From China to Cuba to Vietnam, history teaches the power of a guerrilla movement. In business, too, a guerrilla has a reservoir of tactical advantages that allows the small company to flourish in the land of the giants.

Size, of course, is relative. The smallest automobile company (American Motors) is considerably larger than the largest shaving company (Gillette). Yet American Motors should fight a guerrilla war and Gillette should fight a defensive war.

What's more important than your own size is the size of your competition. The key to marketing warfare is to tailor your tactics to your competition, not to your own company.

Tanks take a beating in Iraq
Not designed for insurgent attacks

Front-page headline from the March 30, 2005, issue of *USA Today*. In business as in warfare, a company using a guerrilla strategy can effectively compete with a larger, more established company.

Guerrilla principle No. 1

Find a segment of the market small enough to defend. It could be small geographically. Or in volume. Or in some other aspect difficult for a larger company to attack.

A guerrilla organization does not change the mathematics of a marketing war. (The big company still beats the small company.) Rather a guerrilla tries to reduce the size of the battleground in order to achieve a superiority of force. In other words, tries to become a big fish in a small pond.

Geography is the traditional way to accomplish this objective. In any given city or town, you can usually find a department store bigger than a Sears, a restaurant bigger than a McDonald's, a hotel bigger than a Holiday Inn.

The local retailer tailors the merchandise, food, or services offered to local tastes. There's nothing new in this notion. It's what a local retailer does almost automatically.

The point is, the would-be successful guerrilla should use the same kind of thinking in other situations where the segments might not be so clearcut.

Rolls-Royce, for example, is a high-priced guerrilla in the automobile business. They dominate the market for cars costing more than $100,000. As a matter of fact, they own it.

Nobody thinks of competing with Rolls-Royce because (1) the existing market is small and (2) Rolls-Royce, at least initially, would have an enormous advantage. The mathematics are on the side of Rolls-Royce.

Did you ever hear of a computer company called Computervision? Well, they're bigger than IBM . . . in CAD (computer-aided design) work stations. This is classic guerrilla strategy—concentrating on a niche or segment of a market that you can defend against the industry leader.

webvan

freshdirect

Fresh Direct is successfully using a strategy that was a total disaster when it was used by Webvan. The difference is that Webvan used a national offensive strategy against the supermarket industry, whereas Fresh Direct picks and chooses its markets using a guerrilla strategy. New York City, for example, was an excellent choice for Fresh Direct because the city's supermarkets are weak, parking space is almost nonexistent, and consumers are stressed out by the time restraints of living in the big city. Fresh Direct's slogan: "Our food is fresh, our customers are spoiled."

In CAD computers, for instance, Computervision holds a 21 to 19 advantage over IBM in share of market. This margin should be a key concern of Computervision's management. They must maintain it at all costs. When a guerrilla begins to lose a battle in his "home territory," the guerrilla will start to go downhill rapidly. More than anything else, a guerrilla needs the credentials that market leadership conveys. Even if the market is small.

In some respects, a guerrilla campaign looks like a flanking attack. You could say, for example, that Rolls-Royce is a high-priced flanker. But there's a critical difference between flanking and guerrilla warfare. A flanking attack is deliberately launched close to the leader's position. The objective of a flanking attack is to bleed or unravel the leader's share.

Mercedes-Benz is a high-price flanking attack against Cadillac. And it did succeed in bleeding business from the General Motors division—so much so that Cadillac launched the Seville in an attempt to defend its turf.

Rolls-Royce is the true guerrilla. While Rolls-Royce, in a literal sense, might take business from someone else, its strategy is not designed to unravel a competitive position. The Rolls-Royce dealer might just as likely be taking business away from a municipal bond sales rep or a jewelry store as another automobile dealer.

How small a market should a guerrilla set its sights on? That's where judgment comes in. Try to pick a segment small enough so that you can become the leader.

The tendency is to do the opposite, to try to grab as big a market as possible. This could be a mistake.

You seldom read about companies that went under because the market they were concentrating on was too small. On the other hand, you often read about companies torn apart by overexpansion, companies that launched too many products in too many markets in too large a geographic area.

Sometimes it's tempting for a guerrilla to change its strategy to a flanking one; in other words, to attempt to increase market share by getting closer to the industry leader and unraveling their position. Why shouldn't Rolls-Royce, for example, introduce a less expensive car and take business from Cadillac, Mercedes-Benz, and BMW?

The key consideration is resources. Does the guerrilla have the resources (in money and organization) to take on increased competition?

Sometimes, yes. More often, no. To take on a larger organization, guerrillas sometimes forget that they must give up their guerrilla stronghold and move out into the open.

Why can't a guerrilla do both? Keep its guerrilla position at the same time that it launches a flanking attack? Why can't Rolls-Royce continue to sell $150,000 cars as well as $50,000 cars designed to flank the Mercedes crowd?

We call this line of thinking the "line extension trap." One name can't support two different concepts. The low-cost Rolls-Royce undermines the position of the high-priced product. And quite often, the low-priced product doesn't sell either because who wants to buy a cheap Rolls-Royce?

That's not just theory. In the thirties Packard introduced the Packard Clipper, a lower-priced version of a high-priced car. The cheap cars sold; the expensive ones didn't. The Clipper was the primary reason the Packard nameplate disappeared into automotive history.

Again, it's a matter of concentration. By its nature, a guerrilla has limited forces to start with. To stay alive, a guerrilla must steadfastly resist the temptation to spread its forces. This just invites disaster.

Guerrilla principle No. 2

No matter how successful you become, never act like the leader. The day the guerrilla company orders its first Cadillac limousine for the chairman of the board is the day the guerrilla company starts to go downhill.

We would have won the war in Vietnam if we could have persuaded the Viet Cong to send their officers to West Point to learn how to fight like we do.

And most guerrilla companies are lucky their leaders didn't go to the Harvard Business School to learn how to market like General Motors, General Electric, and General Dynamics.

That's not to say that the business schools of this world don't produce excellent leaders. They do, for the big companies whose case histories make up the core of their curriculum. But the essence of guerrilla strategy and tactics is the opposite of what's right for the Fortune 500 crowd.

Successful guerrillas operate with a different organization and a different timetable.

New beauty you'll appreciate with your eyes closed
PACKARD CLIPPER 4-DOOR SEDAN $1375

In the late 1920s, Packard was the largest-selling luxury car in America, outselling Cadillac, Pierce-Arrow, and Peerless. But what would you have done when the Great Depression hit in the early 1930s? That's exactly what Packard did, introducing the One-Twenty and later an even cheaper model, the One-Ten. We were mistaken about the Clipper name in the text; the relatively inexpensive Packard Clipper wasn't introduced until 1941. [Note the emphasis on low prices in the Clipper advertisement.] But our point is still valid. Packard might still be around today if it had hunkered down during the Depression and maintained its high-price luxury position.

In Vietnam, only one out of seven soldiers was in a combat troop. The other six were in supply and service functions. The ratio would not be much different in a large corporation. Only a small percentage of employees are on the front lines serving customers.

We went into Vietnam with thousands of cooks, bakers, clerks, chauffeurs, chaplains, public relations officers. The enemy had none of these. Virtually every enemy soldier had a gun which he used against us. A large proportion of our soldiers, on the other hand, were used in managing, supplying, and servicing the needs of our fighting men. (Who's going to cook their hot meals after a hard day in the field?)

(In 1968, when we had 543,000 troops in Vietnam, only some 80,000 were combat soldiers. The rest served in supply and service functions.)

Look how a big company is organized. In a typical case, more than half the employees provide services for other employees. The smaller part of the corporate army is directed outside the company where they are engaged with the real enemy, the competition.

Some corporate employees spend years without ever meeting a customer or seeing a competitive salesperson. These are the "cooks and the bakers" of corporate America.

Guerrillas should exploit this weakness by getting as high a percentage of their personnel as possible on the firing line. Guerrillas should resist the temptation to make up formal organization charts, job descriptions, career paths, and the other accoutrements of a staff-heavy organization. As far as possible, guerrillas should be all line and no staff.

The lean organization is not just a tactic to put a higher percentage of the force into the battle itself. It also dramatically improves the "quickness" of a guerrilla to respond to changes in the marketplace itself.

"Jack be nimble, Jack be quick." Good advice for those Jacks who want to establish strong guerrilla positions.

A guerrilla also can take advantage of its small size to make quick decisions. This can be a precious asset when competing with the big national companies to whom a quick decision means 6 weeks of staff work instead of the usual 6 months.

Guerrilla principle No. 3

Be prepared to bug out at a moment's notice. A company that runs away lives again to fight another day.

This advice is right out of the pages of Che Guevara. Don't hesitate to abandon a position or a product if the battle turns against you. A guerrilla doesn't have the resources to waste on a lost cause. A guerrilla should be quick to give up and move on.

Here's where the advantage of flexibility and a lean organization really pays off. A guerrilla can often take up a new position without the internal pain and stress that a big company goes through.

MCI

MCI started out as a guerrilla and became very successful with a number of attacks against market leader AT&T, including its "friends & family" program. Over time, however, MCI became arrogant and lost its way. In particular, the merger with WorldCom was a disaster.

The lack of titles and staff can also be a big benefit. If you're the executive vice president of Latin America and your company tries to give up on the Latin American market, you're going to fight tooth and nail to hold on to your position. A lot of infighting has to take place before things get changed in a big company.

A small company can change things around without making internal waves.

The flipside of bugging out is bugging in. Guerrillas should use their flexibility to jump into a market quickly when they see an opportunity.

In a small company, one person's hunch can be enough to launch a new product. In a big company, the same concept is likely to be buried in committees for months.

Footwear importer Robert Gamm didn't know what to do with his keys and pocket change while he jogged or played tennis. This inconvenience inspired Mr. Gamm to introduce KangaRoos, athletic shoes with a zippered pocket on the side. Sales quickly shot up to almost $75 million a year.

Sometimes a guerrilla can jump in and take over a territory that a national brand is abandoning for one reason or another. The guerrilla can often move in quickly to fill the void while the market is still there.

When Nalley's Foods found out that Kraft was dropping its imitation mayonnaise, Nalley's came out with a similar product of its own in 9 days. International Rubber, a small Louisville, Kentucky, company that now makes the most expensive radial tires on the market, sells through quality tire dealers who were piqued when Michelin abandoned its one-dealer-per-town franchise system.

Geographic guerrillas

Almost any national product or service can be attacked locally, a classic guerrilla tactic.

Business Week, Fortune, and *Forbes* are strong national business publications. Launching another national business publication would be extremely difficult and expensive. Tens of millions of dollars with scant chance of success.

But city business publications are booming. When the Association of Area Business Publications was formed in 1979, it had 19 member publications. Five years later there were 88.

Michael K. Russell, chairman of American City Business Journals Inc., owner of eight papers, says a weekly can be launched for as little as $750,000.

Crain's Chicago Business is a typical guerrilla success story. Launched in 1978 by Crain Communications, the weekly took 3 years to get into the black. Currently, *Crain's Chicago Business* has 40,000 paid subscribers and an impressive 75 percent renewal rate. Pretax profit margins are said to be a healthy 25 to 30 percent.

A circulation of 40,000 doesn't sound like much compared with *Business Week's* 800,000 circulation. But the big national has only 36,000 subscribers in the metropolitan Chicago area. So in Chicago, at least, Crain's outguns *Business Week.*

A guerrilla doesn't change the mathematics of a marketing war. Rather a guerrilla reduces the size of the battleground in order to achieve a superiority of force.

Almost any industry illustrates the operation of the guerrilla concept. Take banking. In almost any city or state you have small banks that must learn how to compete with the big ones.

In metropolitan New York the big city banks like Chase Manhattan and Citibank dominate the financial battleground. Yet small banks in selected geographic

Crain's Chicago Business now has more than 50,000 subscribers, and the company has introduced similar city business publications in New York, Cleveland, Detroit, Mexico City, and Monterrey, Mexico.

As predicted, PEOPLExpress is no longer with us. In addition to a rapid expansion of routes and schedules, founder Donald Burr bought Boeing 747s and started service to London. In 1985, he bought Frontier Airlines for $300 million. Then he tried to shift his strategy from a no-frills airline to a full-service airline. Facing almost certain bankruptcy, PEOPLExpress was sold to Texas Air in 1987. Contrast Southwest Airlines with PEOPLExpress. Since its inaugural flights in 1971, Southwest has never changed its no-frills strategy. Today, Southwest is the most successful airline in America, worth more on the stock market than the five largest U.S. airlines combined.

areas have done very well using guerrilla tactics. The key is to stress their local approach, starting with their names. Banks like United Jersey and Long Island Trust demonstrate this strategy.

In the airline industry a number of guerrilla operations have gotten airborne. Some are successful, but many collapse when they try to expand their base of operations. Air Florida and Midway are two recent examples.

PEOPLExpress started as a low-end guerrilla, then bought many more planes and opened many more routes. In essence, they changed from guerrilla to flanking warfare at a cost of the flexibility that helped them get off the ground initially. Since they don't have the resources to take on the air forces of American, United, and Delta, the future is definitely cloudy for PEOPLExpress.

Demographic guerrillas

Another classic guerrilla tactic is to appeal to a specific segment of the population—a segment created by carving out a specific category by age, income, occupation, etc.

A publication called *Inc.* represents a typical demographic guerrilla. The first national magazine for the small business owner, *Inc.* has been a phenomenal success since it was launched in 1979. In its first year *Inc.* carried 648 pages of advertising worth almost $6 million, the most successful first year in the history of magazines.

Inc.'s success was based on the shrewd insight of its founder, Bernard A. Goldhirsh. He realized that the national business publications are not what they seem to be. *Business Week* should really be called *Big Business Week*.

With a circulation well under 1 million, *Business Week* reaches only a small percentage of the 5 million corporations in America. *Inc.* was the first to exploit the previously untapped market of small-business people.

Some guerrillas combine both geographic and demographic approaches. *Avenue* magazine, another big marketing success, reaches only upper-income people on the island of Manhattan.

Industry guerrillas

Another classic guerrilla strategy is to concentrate on a specific industry. In the computer business, for example, this strategy is known as vertical marketing.

Some computer companies are selecting an industry—say, advertising or banking or commercial printing—and then designing an entire computer system to solve problems that crop up only in that industry. The systems sometimes include special hardware as well as the software.

Triod Systems of Sunnyvale, California, designed a computer system to solve the complex inventory problems of automotive parts wholesalers. (A typical wholesaler stocks 20,000 parts and finances the inventory with supplier credits.) Now public, Triod brings in revenues well over $100 million a year—substantial sales for a guerrilla operation.

The key to the success of an industry guerrilla is to be narrow and deep rather than broad and shallow. When an industry guerrilla starts to tailor its system to other industries, you can expect trouble to develop.

Product guerrillas

Many guerrillas make money by concentrating on small markets with unique one-of-a-kind products. Their sales never get large enough to tempt the larger companies in the same industry.

In the last 10 years, for example, American Motors has been selling just over 100,000 Jeeps a year. In the same period, General Motors sold 18 times as many Chevrolets. So why should GM launch a Jeep-type product and maybe sell 30,000 or 40,000 more vehicles a year?

Unfortunately, American Motors' military thinking isn't quite as perceptive as GM's. The money AMC makes on Jeeps is thrown away on Alliances, Encores, and other cars designed to compete with Chevrolets.

The most successful passenger car built by AMC is the Eagle, a sedan body on a four-wheel, Jeep-like drive train. In other words, a product that takes advantage of their Jeep position.

Another guerrilla with a unique product is Tandem Computers. Tandem makes fault-tolerant computers for on-line transaction processing. Called the NonStop system, the computer has two processors so that if one fails, the other continues to operate.

TANDEM
NonStop Computing Systems

Tandem Computers continued to do well until 1997, when it was bought by Compaq Computer for $3 billion. The previous year Tandem had revenues of $1.9 billion.

High-end guerrillas

In today's affluent society, there are plenty of guerrillas at the high end of the market: Steinway pianos, Concord watches, Cuisinart food processors, to name three.

The $250 Cuisinart is a typical big-ticket item to rack up big sales. Priced four times higher than models from established companies like General Electric, Sunbeam, and Waring, the Cuisinart has extra features and gadgets to justify the price differential.

Many potential high-end guerrillas hesitate to jump into the market. They worry that their proposed brand names don't have the mystique to justify the extravagant prices they're thinking of charging.

So they compromise by introducing their products at lower prices. Sometimes they cut quality or features to do so. As a result, the new product never does create the mystique or the high sales they want.

They confuse cause and effect. The mystique is not the cause that creates the effect of high demand and high sales. The high quality and high price are the cause that creates the effect (the mystique) which then creates the demand.

High prices create "visibility" in the distribution system. "Hey, look what they're charging for that product," the consumer says. And then asks why. This, of course, creates the opportunity to tell the prospect what the product does to justify the high price.

But you have to be first. Unless you have unlimited resources, which guerrillas almost never have, you have to be the first to occupy the high-end territory. Nobody sold $250 food processors until Cuisinart.

It takes faith and courage to become a high-end guerrilla, faith in the future of your innovation and courage to launch the product with an unknown name.

Potential high-end guerrillas often try to compromise on the name too. Since they plan to charge hefty prices, they feel they need the security of an established name.

Even a mundane product like a cell phone can be a prime target for a high-end guerrilla. The Razr V3 cell phone introduced by Motorola has a list price of $450. Since the phone's introduction in 2004, Motorola has sold more than a million of these ultra-thin devices.

Who would pay more than $3.00 for a cup of coffee? Millions of Americans, that's who. There's always a segment of the market that wants the very best and is willing to pay for it.

This, of course, is another example of the line-extension trap, a constant threat to a company's success. One name can't stand for two different strategies.

There is enormous opportunity at the high-end. But not for $100,000 sports cars or for $10,000 watches. The real opportunity lies at the high end of commodity products.

Who can afford a Ferrari? Not many people. But who can afford to pay $5.00 for a pound of salt (twenty times the normal price)? Almost everybody.

The trick is not selling salt at $5.00 a pound. The trick is finding something to put into the salt to make it worth the price. (The Orville Redenbacher approach to marketing success.)

Developing allies

Developing allies is a common strategy in many industries, especially where the predominant competition consists of hordes of local guerrillas. A typical pattern is the franchisor who attempts to assemble a national chain under a national name, but with local ownership and control. This strategy can be attempted in either of two different ways: top-down or bottom-up.

Top-down organizations develop the entire package and offer it to local business people to run. McDonald's, Pizza Hut, Holiday Inn, Coca-Cola are typical examples. In other words, you develop a concept and then try to recruit an army of guerrillas to make it work.

A more creative approach is the bottom-up organization. These can result in some spectacular successes because a bottom-up operation requires fewer resources to get started.

A typical example is Century 21. The company recruited existing realtors to join the national group which would exchange leads and information. Century 21 was an especially good concept because the sale and purchase of a house often involves moving from the territory of one real estate agent into that of another.

The Leading Hotels of the World, a voluntary group of 195 deluxe hotels, is another successful bottom-up organization. So is Quality Inns, a group of 582 motor inns in North America.

A key question to ask yourself in developing allies is, "Who is the competition?" Sometimes your competition is your neighbor, sometimes not.

Two motels across the street from each other might be fierce competitors—reason enough for one of them to join a chain like Quality Inns. On the other hand, the two motels might be on a Caribbean island where the real competition comes from another island hundreds of miles away. So instead of fighting each other, the two could join forces and promote the values of their island in comparison with the competition's.

In this connection we see more and more joint marketing programs as companies become more sophisticated about isolating the real competition. An understanding of the principles of marketing warfare doesn't necessarily lead to more hostilities. Sometimes just the opposite. One form of cooperation we expect to see a lot more of are alliances: product alliances, regional alliances, demographic alliances, plus many other types.

Leading Hotels of the World continues to make progress. Today it has 420 hotels around the world.

As a general principle, out of every hundred companies, one should play defense, two should play offense, and three should flank.

Obviously, most of the millions of companies in America should be fighting a guerrilla war. Out of every 100 companies, on average, 94 should be guerrillas. Guerrillas can remain successful for long periods of time. They get in trouble only when they try to act like big companies.

The principle of force will encourage guerrillas to band together for self-preservation.

Guerrillas are everywhere

Most of America's 5 million corporations should be waging guerrilla warfare. Big companies may dominate the news, but small companies dominate the landscape.

Take the food industry. There are only a handful of big companies: Kraft, H. J. Heinz, Hershey's. But Kraft is only one of 660 companies that make cheese. Heinz is only one of the 380 companies that package pickles. And there are 864 candy companies in addition to Hershey's.

Most companies should be waging guerrilla warfare. Out of every 100 companies, as a glittering generality, one should play defense, two should play offense, three should flank, and 94 should be guerrillas.

Historical examples provide the best kind of proof in the empirical sciences. This is particularly true of the art of war.

Karl von Clausewitz

11 The cola war

The proper study of war is the study of history. Clausewitz and other writers have made this point repeatedly. Yet marketing people rarely spend much time on marketing history. They're usually too busy keeping up with current events. They see their role as keeping their products in tune with the latest fashions.

Furthermore, marketing histories tend to focus on what happened rather than why things happened. In the absence of a comprehensive theory of marketing, perhaps this is the best that can be done.

One way to test the validity of marketing warfare principles is to look at the history of an industry and then analyze key competitive moves in terms of those principles. We have done so with four different industries. This chapter covers the cola war that has raged for decades between the Coca-Cola armies of Atlanta and the Pepsi-Cola battalions of Purchase, New York.

"The power and influence of big, BIG business . . . rich detail . . . stylistic verve."
—ALA BOOKLIST

THE COLA WARS

The story of the global corporate battle between the Coca-Cola Company and PepsiCo, Inc.

J.C. Louis and Harvey Z. Yazijian

Warfare has become a common metaphor for almost all industries and all categories, including cola.

Cocaine and caffeine

Coca-Cola is a 100-year-old soft drink that started out as anything but soft. Invented by a pharmacist and former confederate officer, John Styth Pemberton, Coca-Cola was introduced as an exotic patent medicine—one that contained both cocaine from coca leaves and caffeine from kola nuts.

Coca leaves were the favorite high of Bolivian Indians who chewed them while working. Hence Dr. Mitchell's Coca-Bola, an early Coca-Cola competitor.

Chewing kola nuts produced much the same effects among West African natives. "Hell seed," claimed certain sects who abstained completely.

Coca-Cola was, first and foremost, a medicine. "A delicious, exhilarating, refreshing, invigorating beverage in addition to being a cure for all nervous afflictions, sick headaches, neuralgia, hysteria, melancholy," said an early advertisement.

By the turn of the century, Coca-Cola's fortunes turned brighter. By 1902, with an ad budget of $120,000, Coca-Cola had become the best-known product in America. The following year, the company took out the cocaine by switching the formula to extract from "spent" coca leaves. (It would take another 70 years for decaffeinated Coke to arrive.)

Fanned by advertising and the temperance movement, Coca-Cola grew rapidly. By 1907 some 825 of the 994 counties of the ex-Confederate states had gone dry. "Great National Temperance Drink," said the ads.

"Holy water of the South," said the pundits up North.

An early ad for Coca-Cola.

In 1915, a designer from Terre Haute, Indiana, came up with a new 6½-ounce bottle that captured the uniqueness of Coca-Cola. Over the years some 6 billion Georgia-green Coke bottles were manufactured.

The new bottle design arrived just in time. Imitators were springing up all over the country. In 1916 alone, 153 imposters were struck down by the courts, including Fig Cola, Candy Cola, Cold Cola, Cay-Ola, and Koca Nola.

In the twenties, Coca-Cola had no real competition. The company's only problem was to increase the consumption of soft drinks, which rose slowly from 2.4 gallons per capita in 1919 to 3.3 gallons in 1929. (Compared with more than 40 gallons today.)

Coca-Cola advertising tried to stimulate consumption. "Thirst knows no season" (1922) and "The pause that refreshes" (1929) are the best examples.

Twice as much for a nickel, too

The depression of the thirties helped Coca-Cola's competition, especially Pepsi-Cola and Royal Crown, get off the ground.

The key concept was the 12-ounce bottle that would sell for the same nickel that would buy only 6½ ounces of Coca-Cola.

Pepsi-Cola hit on the idea in 1934, but it wasn't until 1939 (and the arrival of Walter Mack) that the idea was brought to life.

It was in the form of a radio commercial sung to "John Peel," a traditional English hunting song:

The pause that refreshes

Early on, a leader brand like Coca-Cola should focus on increasing the consumption of the category, as the company did with slogans like "The pause that refreshes," first used in 1929. Today, however, cola consumption is flat or declining, and there's nothing Coca-Cola can do about it. Hence the need for a leader brand to shift to a competitive slogan like "The real thing." (Per-capita soft drink consumption has been declining ever since 1998.)

Pepsi-Cola hits the spot.
Twelve full ounces, that's a lot.
Twice as much for a nickel, too.
Pepsi-Cola is the drink for you.

It was brilliant strategy executed in a spectacular way. It hit the mark, especially with the young. In candy and cola, kids went for quantity rather than quality.

And it was done with a limited advertising budget. In 1939 Coca-Cola spent $15 million on advertising, Pepsi-Cola just $600,000.

Now Coca-Cola was on the spot. They couldn't increase the quantity unless they were willing to scrap a billion or so 6½-ounce bottles. They couldn't cut the price because of the hundreds of thousands of nickel soft-drink machines on the market.

Pepsi-Cola had launched a classic flanking attack at the low end. But it was more than that. Pepsi turned a successful flanking move into an offensive attack against the heart of Coca-Cola's strength.

Offensive principle No. 2: *Find a weakness in the leader's strength and attack at that point.* The folks in Atlanta obviously felt that the Coke bottle itself was their greatest strength. They used it in every ad and even trademarked it. Raymond Loewy dubbed it "the most perfectly designed package in use."

Pepsi-Cola promotion turned that strength into a weakness. That perfectly designed 6½-ounce bottle that fit the hand couldn't be scaled up to 12 ounces. Not unless you had the hand of a 7-foot center for the New York Knicks.

Coca-Cola found a clever way to sell 12-ounce cans without losing the perceptions created by its classic 6-ounce "hour-glass" bottle. The company just used a drawing of the bottle on the can.

During World War II, Pepsi-Cola passed both Royal Crown and Dr. Pepper to become No. 2 to Coca-Cola itself.

What Coke could have done

Defensive principle No. 2: *The best defensive strategy is the courage to attack yourself.* Coca-Cola should have attacked themselves with a second brand long before Pepsi did it to them. And the ideal time to have launched a second brand with a low-cost Pepsi-type theme would have been early in the thirties when the depression was just getting started. (Double Cola, a brand on the market today, would have been a good name to use.)

In concept, this defensive move would have been no different from Gillette's Trac II. And probably equally effective. (Today Gillette has a larger share of the wet shaving market than Coke has of the cola market.)

For a short time after the war, it looked like Coke had lucked out. Economics turned against Pepsi. As the price of sugar and labor rose, so did the price of Pepsi-Cola. First to 6 and then to 7 cents. "Twice as much for a nickel, too" became "twice as much and better, too."

Then Pepsi changed its focus from public consumption in vending machines and soda fountains to private consumption at home, featuring Pepsi's larger bottle. "Be sociable" was the new advertising theme as Pepsi turned its marketing efforts toward the supermarket. That effort paid off.

Ahhh! Same great taste!

Leading brands should never hesitate to block competition by introducing second brands that attack themselves. Double Cola would have been a good conceptual idea for a second brand to block the rise of Pepsi-Cola.

Coke started the decade of the fifties 5 to 1 ahead of Pepsi. As 1960 rolled around, Pepsi had cut that lead in half.

How long could Coca-Cola hold out against the larger-size containers? The moment of truth was the year 1954. Coke's sales fell 3 percent and Pepsi's rose 12 percent.

The following year, Coca-Cola launched a bottle *blitzkreig:* 10, 12, and 26 ounces. As supplies were used up, the 6½-ounce Coke trademark slowly disappeared into the history books.

And every year Coke's advertising theme changed as the company grappled with ways to counteract the Pepsi push. 1956: "Coca-Cola makes good things taste better." 1957: "Sign of good taste." 1958: "The cold, crisp taste of Coke." 1959: "Be really refreshed." These changes were a sure sign of confusion down in Atlanta.

The Pepsi generation

The larger container was the "one" and the Pepsi generation was the "two" in Pepsi's one-two punch which put Coke on the ropes.

Finding weakness in the leader's strength is the key offensive principle of a marketing war. Where is Coca-Cola strong? It was the first cola drink. It had been on the market much longer than Pepsi. This authenticity was an obvious strength of Coke, but it had another less obvious result.

Older people were more likely to drink Coke. Younger people were more likely to drink Pepsi. Furthermore, the larger-size containers also held youth appeal. What adult could swig down a 12-ounce bottle the way a teenager could?

The first expression of this concept was 1961's "Now it's Pepsi for those who think young." By 1964 this idea found wings with the classic "Come alive, you're in the Pepsi generation."

The intent of Pepsi's new strategy was to reposition the competition as "out of step, out of touch, and out of date." Which it did, but it also had another psychological benefit of equal value.

It took advantage of natural sibling rivalry among the target audience. Since more people drank Coca-Cola than Pepsi, older siblings were also more likely to drink Coke. Younger siblings could then express their normal rebelliousness by drinking Pepsi. This strategy works neatly up and down the age ladder. As Coca-Cola buries its customers, new Pepsi customers are being born.

Pepsi also wisely used music, a traditional form of teenage rebellion, as a key component in its strategy. Currently Pepsi uses Michael Jackson and Lionel Richie in its commercials. The teenager sees Lionel Richie and says, "Wow." The adult sees him and says, "Who's Lionel Richie?"

The current Pepsi theme, "The choice of a new generation," is another expression of its youth strategy, which is the key point of attack against the "older" Coca-Cola product.

Yet like most companies, Pepsi Cola frequently tends to lose its strategic way. In the past two decades, Pepsi has used the "generation" idea only about one-third of the

"The choice of a new generation" is how Pepsi's youth-oriented strategy evolved over the years (probably better expressed as "the Pepsi generation"). This is one of the best marketing strategies of all time. A No. 2 brand needs to be the opposite of the leader. In essence, Pepsi told younger people, "You don't want to drink what your parents drank; you're the Pepsi generation."

time. Two-thirds of the time they have backed other campaigns. 1967: "Taste that beats the others cold, Pepsi pours it on." 1969: "You've got a lot to live, Pepsi's got a lot to give." And 1983's placid "Pepsi now!"

For a consumer product, advertising is the brand's most important strategic weapon. It's a mistake to change your strategic direction on an annual basis. You probably should never change until you move your product from one form of marketing warfare to another.

Of course, from a tactical point of view, the words, the pictures, the music can be changed as frequently as necessary. But the strategy, no.

Still, the overall effect of Pepsi's efforts was to steadily erode Coke's leadership. From 2.5 to 1 in 1960 to 1.15 to 1 in 1985.

**It's the real thing.
Coke.**

One of the most effective advertising slogans ever conceived, "The real thing" was first used by Coca-Cola in 1970 and has been used intermittently ever since.

Coca-Cola's comeback attempts

Over the years, Coca-Cola had missed the opportunity to block Pepsi by not introducing a second brand in a larger bottle. "Twice as much for a nickel, too" would have worked just as well for a Coke brand as it did for Pepsi.

Coca-Cola sold soft drinks while Pepsi sold Pepsi. "The pause that refreshes" being a typical example. "Things go better with Coke" being another.

But in 1970 Coca-Cola finally found the best defensive strategy for a leader. That is, leadership itself.

"It's the real thing." By implication, everything else is an imitation of Coca-Cola. Which, of course, is exactly what the other colas are.

"The real thing" strategy also took advantage of the publicity about "Merchandise 7X," the secret formula for Coca-Cola. Since Dr. Pemberton's day you can count on the fingers of one hand the number of people who have known the 7X formula. That kind of publicity is invaluable in capturing the imagination of the cola-drinking public. But the real thing didn't last long. 1975: "Look up, America." 1976: "Coke adds life." 1979: "Have a Coke and a smile."

By 1982 Coke had hit bottom in insipidness with the slogan: "Coke is it."

Even though Coke deep-sixed "the real thing" years ago, they can't kill the idea. Mention "the real thing" and most people will say Coca-Cola. Ask them "Who's it?" and see how many people say "Coke is it."

You know your advertising is on the right track when the media pick up on your theme. Whenever a newspaper or magazine editor has the opportunity to do so, he or she uses "the real thing" to refer to Coca-Cola. The latest book about the company was entitled, as you might have expected, *The Real Thing*. So why isn't Coke using "the real thing" in its advertising? (*Hint:* It's not creative. That is, it's not new and different.)

Royal Crown: too little, too late

Royal Crown, the No. 3 cola, tried to get back in the game in 1969 by hiring Wells, Rich, Greene, the hot advertising agency that year, and launching a major advertising program.

"We're out to kill Coke and Pepsi," said Mary Wells. "I hope you'll excuse the word, but we're really out for the jugular."

Forget the Royal Crown advertising. It's not a factor. You can't go head to head with two big brands like Coke and Pepsi and expect to win. (At the time, Pepsi alone outsold Royal Crown almost 4 to 1. Today it's 10 to 1.)

Royal Crown's moment in the sun was in the thirties when it outsold Pepsi-Cola. That was the time for Royal

Royal Crown cola did a million taste tests to demonstrate that RC cola tastes better than Coca-Cola Classic (57 to 43 percent) and Pepsi-Cola (53 to 47 percent). It didn't matter. You can't win with a better-tasting product. You can win only with a better name and a better strategy that help you create a better perception.

Crown to make its move. By 1969 it was that old story: Too little, too late.

Year after year, Royal Crown's share of the cola market declines. What can a distant No. 3 brand do?

The answer, of course, is to change its mode of warfare and its marketing strategy. The logical choice for Royal Crown is to become a guerrilla. The first principle of guerrilla warfare is to find a segment of the market small enough to defend.

Possibly Royal Crown could establish a geographic position in an area of the country. Possibly in the South, where Royal Crown is at its strongest. If they try to fight a nationwide battle with limited resources, they are bound to be overwhelmed by Coke and Pepsi. As soft drinks proliferate, sooner or later there's going to be no room on the shelf for a No. 3 cola.

Actually there was another option for Royal Crown in the early sixties.

The battle of the bulge

Royal Crown opened the sixties with a powerful flanking move: Diet Rite Cola. It caught the competition by surprise. It was 3 years before Coca-Cola responded with Tab, and Pepsi-Cola with Diet Pepsi.

By the end of the decade Diet Rite was the largest selling diet soft drink. It alone represented almost half of Royal Crown's earnings.

Flanking principle No. 3: *The pursuit is just as critical as the attack itself.* Diet Rite had succeeded with a bold flanking move which Coke and Pepsi helped by contributing 3 years of time. Now it was decision time. Should Royal Crown continue to field a full line of colas? Or concentrate its resources on a winner?

Diet Rite versus Royal Crown? Jeep versus passenger cars? These fundamental strategic decisions never seem to get decided. American management prefers to let the marketplace decide for them. So they try to fight on two fronts with predictable results.

Diet Rite Cola slowly slid into obscurity. A brand that once dominated the diet cola market today has less than 4 percent. Diet Coke alone outsells Diet Rite 14 to 1.

It was an unfair fight. The big two used their Coke and Pepsi profits to finance their diet cola brands. Royal Crown used its Diet Rite profits to finance its futile attacks against the main-line Coke and Pepsi brands.

"Keep the forces concentrated," says Clausewitz. The battle of the bulge once again demonstrates the importance of this key military maxim.

Flanking with the Uncola

Another player to enter the cola game early was Seven-Up. In 1968, the company positioned its lemon-lime beverage as the Uncola. The strategy was to make 7-Up the alternative to Coke and Pepsi. Sales went up 15 percent the first year.

Almost any strong position can be flanked in this manner. As a matter of fact, the stronger the position or share of market, the greater the opportunity to create an alternative. So tea has become the alternative to coffee. BMW

diet RITE

Dropping Royal Crown cola and focusing all of its marketing resources on its winning brand Diet Rite Cola would have been a good marketing move. But in retrospect, Diet Rite is a weak brand because of the generic name. The product would have been much more successful with a better name. (Royal Crown is also a weak name. It sounds like a gasoline.)

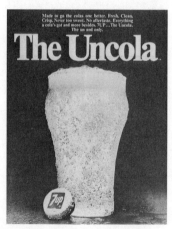

The only 7-Up program that has ever moved the needle is the Un-cola. The company should never have dropped it.

is the alternative to Mercedes-Benz. And 7-Up the alternative to Coke and Pepsi.

Ten years after the Uncola campaign was unleashed, Philip Morris bought Seven-Up for the unprecedented price of $520 million. That was $74 million per "Up."

Fresh from marketing victories with its Marlboro and Miller Lite brands, Philip Morris was determined to do the same with its new 7-Up brand. It doubled the Seven-Up budget to $40 million and launched a campaign which we characterized as "advertising your aspirations."

"America's turning 7-Up," said the ads, but Seven-Up's sales sang a different tune. That year 7-Up was the only soft drink in the top 10 to lose sales. Seven-Up's share of the soft drink market slipped 10 percent.

At that time, Seven-Up's strategy—besides telling America that it was "turning 7-Up"—was one of singing and dancing. This was attacking the colas at their strongest point, singing and dancing. No one sings and dances better than Coke and Pepsi. (Remember "I want to buy the world a Coke"? It even made it into the juke box.)

Looking at the brand from a military point of view, it was obvious why Seven-Up's sales had plateaued and why the "turning 7-Up" strategy wouldn't work. What Seven-Up had done was to create a separate "alternative" position. In doing so, they had taken business from ginger ale, root beer, orange drinks, and the other alternatives to the colas.

Now was the time to switch to offensive warfare, to give Coke and Pepsi drinkers a reason to go "un." Offensive principle No. 1: *The main consideration is the strength of the leader's position.*

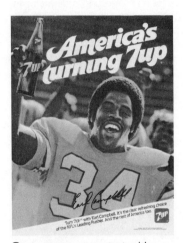

Consumers are not stupid. When they see an advertisement like "America's turning 7-Up," they know it's phony because America is not turning 7-Up.

Where are the colas strong? It has to be the flavor. The cola nut.

Offensive principle No. 2: *Find a weakness in the leader's strength and attack at this point.* Where are the colas weak? The weakness has to be found in the flavor, the cola nut.

If you read a can of Coca-Cola, you find the following ingredients: carbonated water, sugar, caramel color, phosphoric acid, natural flavorings, caffeine.

Caffeine? Sure, all cola drinks contain caffeine. It's in the kola nut. And by federal regulation you can't call Coke a cola unless it contains caffeine.

Who drinks soft drinks? Kids do. It's a two-step distribution process. Parents load up at the supermarket; kids load up at the refrigerator.

The irony of the caffeine situation is the fact that the Food and Drug Administration mandated caffeine content in colas (when it learned that the processing of kola nuts robbed them of their natural caffeine). So Coca-Cola has to buy caffeine from companies like General Foods. Parents that give their kids Coca-Cola may be giving them the same caffeine that was taken out of their Sanka.

What does a dictionary say about caffeine? "A bitter crystalline alkaloid present in coffee, tea, and kola nuts; a stimulant to the heart and central nervous system."

Parents don't want to stimulate their kids. Parents want to calm them down. Kids are hyper enough. (Kid Valium would be a big seller if Hoffmann-LaRoche would market it.) We presented a "no-caffeine" idea to Seven-Up early in 1980. The prototype television commercial said: "You wouldn't give your kid a cup of coffee. Then why give the kid a can of cola which contains just as much caffeine? Give her the Uncola, Uncaffeine soft drink, 7-Up."

"Never," said a marketing vice president when this idea was presented to Seven-Up. "Never will we promote our product that way."

Well, never is not such a long time when you're losing market share. So early in 1982 Seven-Up introduced its "no-caffeine" strategy. "Never had it, never will," said the new 7-Up cans.

But Seven-Up proceeded to make two strategic errors. First, they also introduced a decaffeinated cola called Like. They split their forces and caused consumer confusion. Second, they forgot the Uncola. It wasn't enough to say that Coke and Pepsi contained caffeine and 7-Up didn't. They also needed to remind consumers that 7-Up was the Uncola, the alternative to Coke and Pepsi.

Still, the no-caffeine strategy gave Seven-Up a shot in the sales arm. And Seven-Up moved up from fourth to third place in soft drinks.

It wasn't long before Seven-Up lost its concentration. The no-caffeine strategy was bent to include "no artificial colors."

No artificial colors? What about those delicious (and colorful) flavors of Jello? From cake frostings to Kool-Aid, a kitchen cook depends on artificial colors.

Recently Seven-Up has gone back to the Uncola campaign. That's three major programs in a handful of years. The objective of a marketing war is to create confusion in

Since the book was published, 7-Up changed direction and introduced 7-Up Plus, a product that did contain caffeine. Then they introduced Mixed Berry 7-Up Plus which did not contain caffeine but did contain fruit juice. Not surprisingly, 7-Up sales have continued to decline.

the enemy ranks, not your own. It will be sometime before Seven-Up gets straightened out.

Chaos and confusion in colas

Actually the "no-caffeine" campaign did exactly what a offensive attack should do. It created chaos and confusion in the ranks of Coke and Pepsi.

"Seven-Up ads on caffeine rile industry," said *The Wall Street Journal.* In a formal statement, PepsiCo called Seven-Up's ad campaign "a disservice to the public, since it perpetuates unsubstantiated health concerns by the use of scare tactics." The Pepsi maker said it is "firmly convinced" that caffeine poses no health risk.

The lady from Purchase doth protest too much, methinks. Less than 6 months later PepsiCo introduced Pepsi Free in regular and diet versions.

Others followed suit: Coca-Cola, Royal Crown, Dr. Pepper. Even Sunkist took the caffeine out. (What was caffeine doing in an orange soda?)

Competitors became caffeine-conscious. Brands that never had caffeine in the first place started to say so—Sprite, Canada Dry ginger ale, among others.

We should also mention RC 100. In the entire history of the cola wars, RC 100 rates barely a footnote. Yet RC 100 was the first decaffeinated cola. Introduced by Royal Crown in 1980, the product quickly took off. But in a replay of the Diet Rite Cola situation, RC 100 got smothered by the caffeine products from Coke and Pepsi. It's

RC 100 was the first decaffeinated cola, a fact that no one knows because the product was undermined by a bad name. A new category needs a new name.

In our opinion, Coca-Cola would have been better off if it had never introduced Diet Coke and had instead focused a significant share of its resources on making Tab its diet brand. Before Diet Coke was launched, Tab was the leading diet cola brand, outselling Diet Pepsi by 32 percent.

not enough to be first. You have to be firstest with the mostest.

The battle of the bulge: round 2

The guns of August (1982) were fired at New York's Radio City Music Hall where Coca-Cola launched Diet Coke, the first production to be given the Coke name since the original was introduced in 1886.

No product has ever hit the market with as much initial success. "If there was ever a sure thing in marketing," said *The New York Times,* "Diet Coke seems to be it."

"Diet Coke appears well on its way," predicted *The Wall Street Journal,* "to becoming the second most popular soft drink in the history of the Coca-Cola Co."

"The hottest-selling soft drink in the shortest amount of time ever," said the editor of *Jesse Meyers' Beverage Digest.*

Nor were its Atlanta parents modest when it came to bragging about the achievements of their latest offspring.

"Diet Coke is the most significant new product news in the entire 96-year history of The Coca-Cola Company," said Brian G. Dyson, president of Coca-Cola USA, "and likely the extraordinary event of the soft drink industry in the 1980s."

After all these accolades you'd have to have some nerve to accuse Coke of shooting themselves in the wallet. Yet long term, that's just what they've done.

Sure, short term, Diet Coke is a big success. (So were Diet Rite Cola and RC 100.) Diet Coke seems securely settled in third place after Coke and Pepsi. But at what price?

First of all, Tab. The year Diet Coke was introduced, Tab had a 4.3 percent of the soft drink market. As Diet Coke went up, Tab headed south. In 1984 Tab tumbled to 1.8 percent of the market.

So Coca-Cola did what clients always do when the client makes a mistake. They fired the Tab ad agency and changed the Tab advertising. Can Tab be turned around? No, not unless Coke goes off its diet.

Second of all, Coca-Cola. The year Diet Coke was introduced, Coke had a market share of 23.9 percent which shrank to 21.7 percent in 1984.

So it goes. The gains of Diet Coke are almost matched by the losses of Tab and Coca-Cola itself.

The Pepsi challenge

One other Pepsi strategic move in the mid-seventies deserves comment. Called the "Pepsi challenge," it involved blind taste tests between two unnamed colas. In the tests, tasters preferred Pepsi 3 to 2 over Coke, a fact which was trumpeted in television commercials.

Good strategy? Perhaps, because it exploits a weak point in the competitive product. Since Pepsi is about 9 percent sweeter than Coke, the first taste favors Pepsi. (A product attribute that also supports the Pepsi generation strategy. Nothing can be too sweet for a 12-year-old.)

But not good strategy as a second front to the major Pepsi effort. A No. 2 product can't afford two campaigns. Offensive principle No. 3: *Launch the attack on as narrow a front as possible.*

The Pepsi Challenge
The Pepsi Generation

Pepsi-Cola has wavered between two very good strategies. The company would have been much better off picking one or the other and then sticking with it.

131 YEARS.
★ SEVEN GENERATIONS. ★
ONE RECIPE.
(ENOUGH SAID.)

Every industry is different, but in beverages people like "old." Witness the continuing success of coffee and tea, some of the oldest beverages in the world. In wine, in liquor, in beverages in general, old is usually better than new, as in New Coke. "131 years. Seven generations. One recipe." is how Jack Daniel's positions itself. Jack Daniel's has become the seventh-largest-selling liquor brand in the world.

Prefer New Coke	55%
Prefer Old Coke	19%
No difference	26%

In blind taste tests, consumers preferred New Coke to the original almost three to one.

But then Coca-Cola did the one thing a leader should never do. After years of fighting the Pepsi challenge, Coca-Cola suddenly and publicly changed their formula to match the sweetness of Pepsi-Cola.

Now the real thing was no longer the real thing anymore. In one stroke Coca-Cola had undermined their own position.

The issue was not whether to change the formula or not. The issue was whether or not to announce the change. Most companies make minor formula changes from time to time as had Coca-Cola, most notably the substitution of high-fructose corn syrup for sucrose.

To many companies "new, improved" is a marketing way of life.

What makes the Coca-Cola situation different is its "real thing" position. In a rapidly changing world, the taste of Coca-Cola was a constant that reassured consumers that they weren't getting older. The loss of the Coke bottle was bad enough. Now the formula is gone too.

The return of the real thing

Less than 3 months after the introduction of "New Coca-Cola," a bruised and battered Atlanta army threw in the towel. They announced that the real thing would return with a new name: Classic Coke.

The return of the real thing spells the death of New Coke. We Predict that New Coke will be gone in short order.

Perception is stronger than reality. In spite of the fact that tests showed that New Coke tastes better than old Coke, customers believe otherwise. After all, original Coke is the real thing. How can anything taste better than the real thing?

Perception affects taste in the same way that it affects all human judgment. The battle takes place in the mind. There are no facts in a human mind. There are only perceptions. The perception is the reality.

Whenever you go against your own perception in the consumer's mind, you are bound to lose. Xerox means copiers in the mind, so they could never successfully market a Xerox computer.

Volkswagen means small, durable, reliable cars. So Volkswagen couldn't sell big expensive cars until they put the Audi name on them.

Changing the Coca-Cola formula meant going against its "real thing" perception. Changing it back publicly acknowledges the fact that the company made a mistake. Coca-Cola has undermined its own mental position.

For the first time in its history, Coca-Cola's leadership is at stake. Pepsi has a good opportunity in the near future to take the top spot in the cola category.

The caffeine challenge

Coke's ability to hold off the Pepsi challenge is affected by a development on another front. In an effort to protect itself against 7-Up's "no caffeine" attacks, Coca-Cola launched decaffeinated versions of three of its cola

Prefer New Coke	**13%**
Prefer Old Coke	**59%**
No difference	**28%**

When consumers knew what they were tasting, however, the results were reversed. Consumers now preferred the original to New Coke more than four to one. In cola, in beer, in beverages of all kinds, consumers tend to "drink the label." Expensive wine in an expensive bottle tastes better than cheap wine in a cheap bottle, even if there is no difference in how the wine actually tastes.

It took us 54 years to grow one this big.

Drivers wanted

They never learn. The Volkswagen Phaeton (list price: $66,515 to $98,215) has been a disaster. As one reviewer said, "There are two minor faults. The Volkswagen badge on the grill and the one on the trunk."

When you head down the slippery slope of line extension, things always go from bad to worse. Back in 1985, Coca-Cola had eight cola products. Now it has fourteen, including such weirdos as Coca-Cola Zero, Diet Coke with Splenda, and Coca-Cola C2. Under consideration is a coffee-flavored cola, a product that flopped when Pepsi-Cola test-marketed it in 1996. It's no wonder that the fizz has gone out of the Coca-Cola Company.

brands. So now Coke has eight cola products and a lot of chaos and confusion. (Classic Coke, New Coke, Cherry Coke, Diet Coke, Tab, Caffeine-Free New Coke, Caffeine-Free Diet Coke, and Caffeine-Free Tab).

Coca-Cola apparently doesn't recognize the dangers of decaffeinated colas. Look at coffee. As sales of decaffeinated brands go up, coffee consumption in total goes down.

After a while, people won't drink Coke because it contains caffeine and they won't drink caffeine-free Coke because it's not "the real thing."

The combination of the formula change and the decaffeinated brands bodes problems for the folks in Atlanta. Even the consumer who sticks with Coca-Cola through its midlife crisis will have trouble ordering the product, as this recent conversation at a soda fountain indicates:

"Give me a Coke."

"Would you like a Classic Coke, a New Coke, a Cherry Coke, or a Diet Coke?"

"I'd like a Diet Coke."

"Would you like a regular Diet Coke or a caffeine-free Diet Coke?"

"The hell with it. Give me a 7-Up."

Many assume that half efforts can be effective. A small jump is easier than a large one, but no one wishing to cross a wide ditch would cross half of it first. Karl von Clausewitz

The beer war

Beer marketers have been turned on by military thinking for a long time. The inner sanctum of Anheuser-Busch's marketing efforts is a ninth-floor conference room at headquarters known as "the war room." Inside, the walls are plastered with maps on which black arrows point up or down to reflect the performance of the company and its competitors.

Since World War II, most of the black arrows at Anheuser-Busch have been pointing up.

The breakthrough by Budweiser

After the war, the beer industry went through an unsettling period. The No. 1 brand was Schlitz, the beer that made Milwaukee famous.

But after you've seen Paree, Milwaukee doesn't seem so famous anymore. So down at the American Legion Hall and the VFW, the boys started experimenting with other brands, notably Budweiser, the king of beers.

In May 1979, many experts, including the editors of this magazine, were predicting that Miller would crush Budweiser in the "beer wars." It didn't happen, for reasons explained in this chapter.

One of the reasons for Budweiser's success is the name itself. Budweiser, especially its nickname "Bud," is just an easier name to say than Schlitz. Also, the name Schlitz has some negative connotations. Kids in Milwaukee used to say, "It may be Pabst in the glass, but it's Schlitz in the pants."

The lead changed back and forth. In 1951 and 1952, it was Schlitz on top. In 1953 and 1954, it was Budweiser. In 1955 and 1956, Schlitz again.

These were the crucial years when half efforts were not good enough. The truth is, the victory could have gone to either brand. A few million extra dollars for advertising might have tipped the scale. Yet too often companies in these situations fail to appreciate the enormous long-term advantages of even a small margin of difference in a single year.

In these crucial periods, top management tends to ask the wrong questions about a proposed increase in the advertising budget. They tend to ask: "What's the return on the investment?"

Instead they should ask: "How much do we have to spend to ensure victory?"

Clausewitz points out that sometimes the margin between winning and losing a war is a "trifling difference between victor and vanquished in killed, wounded, prisoners, and artillery lost on the field of battle itself."

In 1957 Budweiser grabbed the lead again, by 1½ percentage points, and was never headed. What once was a horse race has turned into a rout. Today Budweiser outsells Schlitz 20 to 1.

Some beer people claim that Budweiser's victory was the result of an inferior product produced by Schlitz. And it is true that Schlitz was the talk of the industry in the late sixties when it built highly efficient breweries and cut its brewing cycle, a move that purists claim hurt the taste of the beer.

Maybe so, but that was a decade after Schlitz had already lost its leadership to Budweiser. And the history of marketing (as well as warfare) shows that when the other side has the upper hand and the momentum, things are going to go from bad to worse. The rich get richer, the poor get poorer.

The assault by Heineken

Compared with Bud's breakthrough, Heineken's victory was accomplished almost without casualties. The difference, of course, was that Budweiser's gains came entirely at Schlitz's expense. Heineken had virtually no competition.

The first major imported beer to land in the United States after the war, Heineken easily established a foothold in the market. It was a typical flanking assault against no defense. But the most important part of Heineken's strategy came next.

Flanking principle No. 3: *The pursuit is just as critical as the attack itself.* In the early years, Heineken consistently poured substantial dollars into marketing and especially into advertising. Year after year, Heineken outspent its imported rivals.

The first major brand to take a swing at Heineken was Lowenbrau of Munich. Packaged in extremely attractive blue-, green-, and silver-wrapped bottles, Lowenbrau launched a spectacular advertising campaign that is still talked about today.

If they ran out of Lowenbrau.....order champagne.

A great advertisement for the wrong brand.

"If they run out of Lowenbrau . . . order champagne." It was dramatic, eye-catching, and memorable, but exactly the wrong campaign for Lowenbrau.

Comparing beer with champagne (a thought lifted from Miller High Life) would have been fine for Heineken because it broadens the market for a high-priced imported beer.

Lowenbrau's problem was not the size of the market. That could come later. Lowenbrau's problem was Heineken. Lowenbrau should have launched an offensive attack to take over the territory. First, you have to own the market before you start a market-building program.

Offensive principle No. 2: *Find a weakness in the leader's strength and attack at that point.* Heineken was an imported beer—that was the strength—but where was it imported from?

Holland. That was the weak point. Holland is known for windmills, cheese, and canals, but not for beer.

France for wine; Germany for beer. These were established positions in the mind of the American drinker. They could have been used by Lowenbrau (or another German beer for that matter) to exploit the weakness in the Heineken defense.

Offensive principle No. 3: *Launch the attack on as narrow a front as possible.* Lowenbrau should have said: "Now that you've tried the best beer from Holland, try the best from Germany." Forget the hops, forget the malt, forget the tender loving care of brewmasters with a 400-year tradition of quality. Strike at the competition with a narrow, focused attack that exposes and exploits the competition's weakness.

Why is it, a beer drinker will say, that the best beer is brewed in Germany, but the No. 1 imported brand comes from the Netherlands?

Heineken has done a good job, the marketing expert will reply. True, but that's not the real answer.

The real answer is that Heineken reigns supreme, the No. 1 brand with 40 percent of the imported beer market . . . by default.

Later, Miller Brewing bought the rights to the Lowenbrau name and started to brew the beer in America. The target of the new Lowenbrau strategy: Michelob from Anheuser-Busch.

Anseuser didn't hesitate to strike back. It slowed Lowenbrau's growth by successfully charging that the beer was deceptively advertised and priced as an import when it was, in fact, domestically brewed.

The sword that Lowenbrau failed to pick up when they were an import was ultimately used against them when they became a domestic brand.

Currently, a German brand is trying to pick up the lance left unused by Lowenbrau.

"The most famous word in the German language . . . Beck's," says a typical television commercial. But Beck's has a number of obstacles.

Beck's is late. Heineken has built an enormous lead. Beck's is a weak German name compared with the array of authentic-sounding German names in the market: Schlitz, Pabst, Budweiser, Busch, Heileman, Blatz, Schaefer, Meister-Brau. All German-sounding and all brewed in America.

A dramatic example of how to use a country-of-origin position against a market leader is Barilla pasta. Three years after it was introduced into the U.S. market with the theme "Italy's #1 pasta," Barilla became the No. 1 pasta in America. Not bad, considering the competition: Ronzoni, Mueller's, Creamette, San Giorgio, and American Beauty, among others. The previous market leader (Ronzoni) was owned by Hershey Foods, a formidable marketing machine. Furthermore, Barilla sells for 5 to 10 percent more than the competition. Ironically, Barilla the product, as opposed to Barilla the brand, is made in Ohio.

Yet in spite of those weaknesses, Beck's is now the No. 3 imported brand. Which shows what can be done by exploiting the weakness of the leader.

Third place is a long way from being first and enjoying the fruits of leadership. Heineken rolls along, outselling Beck's 5 to 1.

Sooner or later, the leading American brewer, Anheuser-Busch, would have to respond to the Heineken invasion.

The counterattack by Anheuser

The classic response by leaders is "me too." In other words, Anheuser could make a deal with a European brewer (preferably German) to import one of their brands. This is the classic blocking strategy, defensive principle No. 3.

Unfortunately, Anheuser waited too long for that kind of blocking strategy to work. It wasn't until 1963 that they finally made a move designed to counter the Heineken threat.

What they did was both simple and brilliant. To go against the first high-priced imported beer, Anheuser-Busch launched the first high-priced American beer. Then they gave it a high-priced name, Michelob. And to burn in the idea, they gave Michelob a high-priced bottle. (And, of course, a high-priced price, an obvious move often overlooked by companies who want to have it both ways.)

"First class is Michelob," said the ads. The beer you drink in the front of the airplane. Then onto "Weekends are made for Michelob." (You want to drink a little something better on the weekends, don't you?)

Michelob has been very successful and, just as important, very profitable. At its peak in 1980, Michelob had almost 6 percent of the U.S. beer business. Michelob not only outsold Heineken, it sold twice as much beer as all the imports combined.

Then Michelob started to decline, but that story comes later.

The rise of Miller

In 1970 Philip Morris bought Miller Brewing, and the beer world has never been the same.

It might be hard to imagine, but in that year Miller was in seventh place in the beer business, outsold by Anheuser-Busch, Schlitz, Pabst, Coors, Schaefer, and Falstaff.

But Miller had two things going for them: Philip Morris money and a clear, consistent strategy.

The target was Budweiser. Like all leaders, the King of Beers was all things to all people. Using Napoleon's favorite tactic when faced with an enemy who spread his defenses, Miller struck at the middle of the line, the heart of the beer market.

"Welcome to Miller Time," said the television commercials. Miller Time was the blue-collar equivalent of the white-collar cocktail hour. You work hard, you deserve a reward, the Miller messages implied.

Joe Sixpack, the heavy beer drinker, responded. But not right away. It took 3 years for Miller sales to turn around, even though the brewer was spending almost twice as many advertising dollars per barrel as the rest of the industry.

(This slow response to advertising is typical of "personal" products like beer, cigarettes, cola. When you drink a brand of beer in a restaurant or bar, you're not only quenching your thirst, you're making a statement about yourself. You have to feel comfortable about a brand before you're willing to make a public statement. That can take time.)

Once the "working man" concept took hold, Miller blasted past Falstaff, Schaefer, Coors, Pabst, and Schlitz to become the No. 2 brand in the country.

Ultimately Budweiser was forced to respond. "For all you do, this Bud's for you," said the King of Beers in a variation of Miller's work-reward theme.

Miller's success with the blue-collar crowd was ironic in view of the fact that the brand originally had a genteel position. Miller High Life, the Champagne of Beers, the label says.

High Life? Nobody called the brand High Life. People look at labels but they don't read them anymore. The brand was called Miller. That's what the radio and television said. Welcome to Miller Time. Not hello to High Life Hour.

There was no problem in taking a country club brand and moving it into the neighborhood bar. (Going in the other direction would have been much more difficult.) The problem was the name. The fine distinction between what the label said and what the beer drinker asked for was going to cause Miller a giant hangover in the years to come.

The launch of Lite

In 1975, Miller Brewing introduced Lite beer. "Everything you always wanted in a beer . . . and less."

Lite was a classic flanking move. It also caught the trend toward lighter products in other categories. Wine instead of liquor, for example. And it followed the principles of flanking to the letter.

1. An uncontested area.   There were no national "light" beer brands. A few regional or guerrilla brands existed. Some light brands had even been launched and failed. Gablinger's, in particular, was a highly publicized flop. (Beer drinkers take their brands seriously. The advertising can be humorous—as was Lite's—but the product cannot. Gablinger's just isn't a serious name for a brand of beer.)

2. Tactical surprise.   Lite took the competition totally by surprise. There was no test-marketing, no rumors in the press. Bang! Lite was introduced and rolled out nationally as rapidly as possible. It took a year for Schlitz to respond with Schlitz Light. And 2 years for Anheuser-Busch Natural Light to roll out.

3. The pursuit.   Miller saturated the airwaves with Lite advertising, spending four times the industry's per-barrel average. And Miller never backed off. To this day, Miller continues to dominate the category with heavy Lite advertising. The competition dictated the need for this relentless pursuit of the beer drinker's mind. Three years after Lite's launch, there were 22 other light brands on the market.

The day before the launch of Lite beer, we were riding in a taxi with a Miller Brewing executive. "Look at the paper tomorrow," he said. "We're doing everything you recommended in your positioning articles." So we looked and there it was: a full-page newspaper advertisement announcing the arrival of the first light beer. It was probably the most effective product launch ever, except for one thing: the name. Legally, Miller Brewing could protect the Lite name, but it couldn't prevent other brewers from using the generic Light name. So to differentiate Lite from all the other Lights, Miller renamed the product Miller Lite, which turned out to be a major mistake because it undermined its regular Miller High Life brand.

The industry sees the light

The first major brewer to try to jump into Lite's pool was Schlitz. They jumped in with both feet, spending almost as many advertising dollars on their brand as Miller.

Schlitz even paid $500,000 to tough guy James Coburn to say two words in their TV commercials. Unfortunately for Schlitz, that was one word too many.

"Schlitz Light," said Coburn. Now the brand was committed to a line extension strategy. "Concentrate," says Clausewitz, but American marketers weren't paying attention to the Prussian.

The results were all too predictable. Schlitz Light was soon replaced as a Lite challenger by Anheuser-Busch Natural Light. A serious name, but also a mouthful. So Anheuser-Busch hired the master of malapropism Norm Crosby to tell people. "Ask for a Natural. Don't get misconscrewed."

Making fun of the brand name is a sure sign of name weakness. (What do Isuzus do? How's your old Isuzu? Two ad headlines for a Japanese car that you knew wasn't going to make the grade in America.) And sure enough, Natural soon fell far behind.

One brewer was yet to be heard from. One brewer who held a potentially winning ticket in the light beer sweepstakes.

The brewer was Adolph Coors Company in Golden, Colorado. The brand was Coors, brewed with pure Rocky Mountain spring water in the world's largest brewery.

Coors was the most successful of the regional guerrillas, which included, among others, Olympia in the North-

---

SCHLITZ LIGHT

At the time of the introduction of Schlitz Light, the brewer's core brand Schlitz was the third-largest-selling beer in America. Not only was the introduction of Schlitz Light a mistake, but the line extension helped to destroy the Schlitz brand.

Natural Light is a lousy name, but the brand today is the fifth-largest-selling beer in America, with a market share of 4.2 percent. Why? One reason is that it's the only light beer with a unique name. That is, it's not a line extension of a regular beer. (Amstel Light is the only imported light beer with a unique name; not surprisingly, it became the largest-selling imported light beer. So what is Heineken, the owner of Amstel Light, doing next? That's right. Heineken Light.)

west, Heileman Old Style in the Midwest, Dixie in the South, Rheingold, Schaefer and Ballantine in the East, Utica Club and Genesee in New York State, Iron City in Pittsburgh.

Coors had achieved an incredible mystique. Sold only in 12 western states, Coors was the market leader in 9 of those states.

Celebrities consumed Coors: Paul Newman, Clint Eastwood. Gerald Ford drank it. Henry Kissinger brought cases of Coors back to Washington each time he made a trip to California. "The most chic brew in the country," said *The New York Times*.

Colorado Kool-Aid

Coors was already a light beer. (There are fewer calories in Coors regular beer than there are in Michelob Light.) Denver locals used to kid the product by asking for a "Colorado Kool-Aid."

Even the Coors can said "America's Fine Light Beer."

The arrival of Lite handed Coors a once-in-a-lifetime opportunity and also promised to solve a problem.

The problem was the pressure created for a regional brand like Coors by the big national brands with big national television programs. The number of brewers was steadily shrinking. Following the repeal of Prohibition, there were 786 brewers in America. Today there are about 40 left.

New York City once had 121 breweries. Today there is one. Chicago used to have 45. Today none.

Sold only in the West, Coors beer is smuggled to the East. Henry Kissinger drinks it. So does Paul Newman, though he would abhor the Coors family's politics.

By Grace Lichtenstein

No beer has received as much favorable publicity as Coors. This four-page article in the *New York Times Magazine* raved about the brew.

"America's Fine Light Beer" said the label on a can of Coors Regular, until the brewer launched Coors Light. Then the line mysteriously disappeared.

Before the launch of Coors Light, we made a presentation to Coors management. Our advice: Don't launch a light beer; instead, take advantage of the runaway success of Lite beer from Miller. Position the existing Coors brand as the original light beer, using Western imagery and the theme "pioneer in light beer."

In 1960 the top six brewers had 37 percent of the market. Today they have 92 percent.

The pressure to make Coors a national brand, with the cost-saving advantage of national advertising, was intense. The arrival of Lite created the opportunity. "Power used at the right moment against the right adversary," says Clausewitz, "brings more power."

Coors could ride to the top in the wake of Lite's success and then exploit a weakness in Lite's strength, the key principle of offensive warfare. In other words, Coors had the opportunity to switch from a guerrilla strategy to an offensive strategy.

The hardest type of move a company can make is changing directions. It's unsettling to employees, dealers, and distributors who are used to a seamless unrolling of the carpets of time. At critical junctures when you must change directions, marketing warfare principles can help clarify the issues involved.

Coors had all the weapons in place to seize the "original light beer" position. (An even more poetic expression of that idea is "the pioneer in light beer," a concept which we presented to Coors marketing management in 1978.)

The pioneer idea took advantage of Coors' western heritage, its Rocky Mountain location, even the rugged individualism of the founder and his family.

Up till that time, Coors had done almost no advertising. They had kept their light beer in the dark. The Lite campaign gave Coors a perfect launching pad for unveiling the secret of their success.

But Coors decided otherwise and instead launched Coors Light, a carbon copy of the 23 other light beers on the market. The excuse was that "the public doesn't relate to Coors as already being a light beer." The point was, nobody had told the public. (Who reads the label? In addition to America's Fine Light Beer, the label also said "Coors Banquet." Even Henry Kissinger probably didn't know that Banquet was a Coors name.)

Now Coors had two brands headed for national distribution with two advertising programs to support. Except for Miller, nobody had ever built two big brands on one big beer name.

The weakness of Lite

In a print-oriented world, Lite was a good name for a lower-calorie beer. Unfortunately for Miller, we live in a broadcast world.

On radio and television the sound of the word is more important than how it reads in type. Also in the natural habitat of the beer drinker, the corner bar, the sound of the brand is crucial.

"Bartender, give me a Lite."

"How do you spell that, sir—capital L-i-t-e or lower-case l-i-g-h-t?"

"Never mind, make it a Miller."

As time went on and Lite became more successful, "Make it a Miller" came to mean Miller Lite, not Miller High Life.

The TV advertising wasn't helping by calling the product Lite beer from Miller. Nowhere on the front of the can does it say Miller, only Lite. On the side is a small

Miller trademark with the usual small type that says "Miller Brewing Co., Milwaukee, WI."

One name cannot stand for two different brands. Sooner or later, one way or the other, Miller was going to have to pay the piper for its Lite mistake.

It was later rather than sooner and it was High Life rather than Lite that had to pay the price. In 1979, 4 years after Lite's introduction, Miller High Life hit its peak. In that year High Life was only 21 percent behind Budweiser.

The fall of High Life

Slowly at first and then more rapidly, Miller High Life started to fall behind Budweiser: 32, 40, 49, 59, and finally, in 1984, 68 percent behind the King of Beers. This meant that Budweiser was outselling Miller High Life more than 3 to 1.

The point of no return was 1983 when Miller Lite passed Miller High. Now Miller really meant Lite, in sales as well as in the neighborhood bar.

The press seemed to be stumped. "Miller tackles beer mystery," said *The New York Times* in a typical story about the troubles of High Life. No one seemed to see the linkage between the two brands.

In the military sense, what Miller had done was to flank itself. By using the same name on both products (if only accidentally), the flanking attack undermined their own position instead of the position of Budweiser. "We have met the enemy and they is us," said Pogo.

Out in Trenton, Ohio, is a brand-new $450 million Miller brewery that has never brewed a barrel of beer—a silent memorial to the folly of flanking yourself.

When you flank yourself, the outcome has to be one of two possibilities, both of which are no-win situations.

Either you can successfully flank yourself and destroy the base brand, which is what happened at Miller, or you can protect the base brand and end up with an unsuccessful, but expensive, flanking move.

Line extension is like a teeter-totter. One name can't stand for two different products. When one goes up, the other goes down.

One reason line extension is so insidious is that the long-term effect is clearly the opposite of the short-term effect.

In the short term, line extension is almost always a success, as Miller Lite was. (Diet Coke is another example.) But in the long term, line extension is usually a loser's strategy.

It's like alcohol. In the long term, alcohol is a depressant on the central nervous system. But in the short term, the effects can be just as euphoric as the case movements of Diet Coke.

Yet Miller seems to have missed the linkage or connection between its two Miller brands. To try to save the High Life brand, Miller did the thing clients usually do. Miller hauled its advertising agency out and publicly court-martialed it, presumably for dereliction of duty.

The new agency promptly came up with "Miller's made the American way."

One of the many advertising themes used to try to save the Miller brand was "Made the American Way." Most beer drinkers, however, associate beer with German brewing traditions. That's why the most successful beer brands brewed in America have German names.

Which Miller? Lite or High Life? The television commercials don't say. They show the can, which nobody reads, not even the announcer on the TV commercials.

Miller is in a box. They don't want to say "High Life" because it isn't a working-class name. How many beer drinkers are going to belly up to the bar and say, "Give me a High Life"?

You'd think what happened to Miller would serve as a warning to the rest of the industry. Guess again.

The charge of the light brigade

One after another, the beer industry fell all over themselves trying to imitate Miller.

In addition to Schlitz and Schlitz Light, Coors and Coors Light, the beer barons came up with Michelob and Michelob Light, Etc. and Etc. Light.

Let's look at what happened to each of these self-flankers.

Schlitz Light was the second major brand into the light category. Normally, this headstart should have given Schlitz a big advantage. It didn't. Schlitz alone sold 24 million barrels in 1976, the year Schlitz Light was launched.

Today, Schlitz and Schlitz Light together sell less than 3 million barrels. It was a totally successful flanking move. Both brands were destroyed.

Even when you're successful, you're not. Take Coors Light, which is successful. The year it was launched, Coors Light sold 1.6 million barrels. Every year sales have gone up, reaching 4.5 million in 1984. Currently Coors Light is second only to Miller Lite.

Terrific, but what happened to regular Coors? Sales have been going down. What did they expect from a successful Coors Light flanking attack?

As a matter of fact, Coors sold more beer in 1976, when they had one brand in 12 states with $2 million worth of advertising, than they did in 1984, when they had two brands in 44 states and $33 million worth of advertising. Another example of shooting yourself in the pocketbook.

Michelob matches the Miller experience. Three years after the Michelob Light introduction, the sales of regular Michelob peaked. Then every year since, Michelob declined. Solution: Fire the agency.

Michelob Light peaked the following year and stayed on a plateau. Taken together, both brands have declined 4 years in a row, hardly a testimonial to the effectiveness of line extension. And the worst may be yet to come.

Take Budweiser and Bud Light. Anheuser-Busch was lucky. Bud Light has been, comparatively speaking, a disappointment. So far sales of Bud Light have never exceeded 10 percent of the King's. And not that Anheuser hasn't tried. The brewer is spending $50 million a year to advertise Bud Light. That's nine times as much per barrel as they spend on the base brand.

Budweiser continues to barrel along, outselling the No. 2 brand (Miller Lite) by 2½ to 1. That's in spite of the Bud Light ambush.

How about Etc. and Etc. Light? There's no evidence the beer industry has bought our line-extension message.

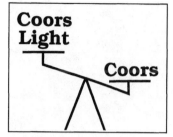

As Coors Light went up in sales, Coors Regular went down. Today, Coors Light outsells the regular four to one.

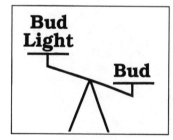

It took awhile, but the same phenomenon happened to Budweiser. As Bud Light went up in sales, Budweiser Regular went down. Bud Light passed Budweiser in 2001 and now outsells it by 37 percent.

As you might have expected, Coors Extra Gold went nowhere, although Coors Light is now the third-largest-selling beer in America. Why is it that marketing people cannot leave well enough alone? We guess they fall in love with the thrill of a new brand launch. It's how they make their mark. Furthermore, does the beer industry need all these line extensions? Per-capita consumption of beer has actually declined in the last two decades, from 24.3 gallons in 1980 to 21.7 gallons today.

Quite the contrary. They continue to lighten up their brands.

Sects that assemble on mountain tops on predicted days of doom to await the end of the world do not come down on the morrow shaken in their ideas. They come down from the mountain with renewed faith in the mercifulness of the Almighty.

When a beer brand doesn't sell, the brewer doesn't come back from the marketplace and blame the name. The brewer blames the product or the advertising. It's just further proof of the deeply held belief that truth will out. "There must have been something wrong," they surmise, "with the taste of the beer or the creativity of the advertising."

"Those who cannot remember the past," said George Santayana, "are doomed to repeat it."

The charge of the heavy brigade

Currently the beer industry is getting revved up to make the same mistake . . . in the opposite direction.

The first candidates for the heavy brigade are Michelob Classic Dark and Coors Extra Gold. Both fall into the classic line-extension trap.

Coors, in particular, should know better. A No. 5 brewer can't afford two national brands, let alone three.

Let us not hear of generals who conquer without bloodshed. If a bloody slaughter is a horrible sight, then it is ground for paying more respect to war.   Karl von Clausewitz

The burger war

In 1984 McDonald's alone spent more than a quarter of a billion dollars on television advertising. That's almost $685,000 a day, $29,000 an hour. You have to sell a lot a burgers to get that kind of money back.

How did such a mammoth enterprise get started? The story begins with the coffee shop, an institution popular in every hamlet and town across America.

Usually a mom-and-pop institution with a counter and six or seven tables, the coffee shop was a name that didn't do justice to the range of food and drink available. You could have ham and eggs, a bacon and lettuce sandwich, an ice cream sundae. And, of course, a hamburger or cheeseburger and french fries.

Each city or region had its specialties. In Philadelphia, the cheesesteak sandwich. In Boston, clam chowder. In the South, grits. It was a marketing war where all the combatants were guerrillas who jealously guarded their turf. (Guerrilla principle No. 1: *Pick a segment of the market small enough to defend.*)

The first McDonald's was a big success. Unfortunately, potential competitors did not go down to the front and observe the action. They waited to launch competitive chains until McDonald's was firmly established. To block competitors, you have to act early.

Enter McDonald's

The business was going to change radically a few short years after Ray Kroc opened his first McDonald's in Des Plaines, Illinois.

What Kroc succeeded in doing was launching an offensive attack against the local coffee shop and then rapidly expanding the operation to do it on a national scale.

In its time, the coffee shop sold almost anything that was simple, easy, and inexpensive to prepare. In a military sense, the line was extended and hence weak.

Kroc made the obvious choice. He struck at the middle. (What was the most popular item on the coffee shop menu? The hamburger and its second cousin, the cheeseburger.)

The burger chain was born. Given no competition (except the weak coffee shops) and his driving ambition, Kroc rapidly expanded his chain. He even borrowed money at exorbitant rates to finance his dream.

More than anything else, this early expansion ensured McDonald's success and allowed it to dominate the developing burger industry. Today McDonald's outsells Burger King, Wendy's, and Kentucky Fried Chicken combined.

To explain McDonald's success, marketing experts love to describe the company's strict standards and procedures, its fanatical devotion to cleanliness, and the intense training given franchise owners at McDonald's ,Hamburger University in Elk Grove, Illinois. (Each graduate is made "Bachelor of Hamburgerology with a minor in French Fries.")

These are luxuries of leadership made possible by the principle of force. McDonald's is the leader because it was first on the burger scene and stayed that way by rapid expansion.

You can't become the leader in the burger war by cooking a better hamburger. You can stay the leader, however, even if you don't cook a better burger. Leadership gives you the luxury of time to correct any problems that might develop.

Back in the seventies, a confidential McDonald's document bluntly admitted that according to public-opinion research, "Burger King's quality is considered to be significantly higher than McDonald's."

Many marketing myths develop because the press looks for reasons to explain a leader's success. For ethical reasons, we can't seem to accept the explanation that McDonald's was first and applied the most pressure: the raw application of the principle of force. It's much more satisfying to suggest that Hamburger University did it. Or Ronald McDonald. Or the dancing floor-moppers in the television commercials.

Good leaders don't discourage such speculation; they encourage it. They know that good morale creates momentum that helps a winning army continue to win.

In the words of George C. Scott as Patton, "Now we have the finest food, equipment, the best spirit, and best men in the world. You know, by god, I actually pity those poor bastards we're going up against."

This is leadership, not strategy. "We couldn't do it without you," says the leader.

McDonald's continues to use its first trademark, the Golden Arches. Burger King, on the other hand, spent millions to introduce an italicized version of its classic "hamburger" trademark. What's Burger King's strategy to compete with the overwhelming power of Mickey D's? We don't know; do you? Don't spend your money to change uniforms, spend your money to give your troops better weapons.

"We could," says the strategist who hopefully keeps his opinion to himself. Or her opinion to herself.

Marketing managers continue to confuse the two, which doesn't damage the leader. The difference between leadership and strategy, however, tends to corrupt the thinking at Hardee's, Burger Chef, and all the other guerrilla players in the burger war.

Marketing myths create false illusions. If we could only develop a better hamburger than Burger King or better service than McDonald's, we could . . . and the dreaming goes on and on.

In the burger war, as in other marketing wars, the product is a vehicle to drive the strategy home. You shouldn't think in terms of betterness, only in terms of differentness.

Burger King's way

The first chain to apply an effective strategy against McDonald's was Burger King.

After McDonald's became the largest national fast-food chain, they were no longer on the offensive, they were on the defensive. The opportunity to apply offensive strategy fell on the No. 2 chain, Burger King.

Offensive principle No. 2: *Find a weakness in the leader's strength and attack at that point.* McDonald' strength was the hamburger, its uniformity, instant delivery, and the inexpensiveness.

Or as the advertising said about the top of the line, the Big Mac: "Two all-beef patties, special sauce, lettuce, cheese, pickles, onions on a sesame seed bun." This was normally said in one big mouthful: "Twoallbeefpattiesspecialsaucelettucecheesepicklesonionsonasesameseedbun." (In print, McDonald's added a little TM to indicate that this was a registered trademark.)

What's the weakness inherent in that strength? Obviously, it's the assembly-line system McDonald's uses to deliver inexpensive hamburgers quickly. If you wanted anything special, you had to wait in a separate line while a food attendant went in the back and fiddled with the system.

In the early seventies, Burger King came up with a strategy to exploit this weakness. "Have it your way," said the ads, "without the pickles, without the relish." Or anyway you wanted it.

At Burger King, the advertising promised, you wouldn't be treated like an outcast if you asked for something special.

And Burger King's sales responded. "Have it your way" effectively differentiated the two chains in terms of customer service and condiments. Note, too, that McDonald's was squeezed. It couldn't afford to tamper with its finely tuned system in order to match the Burger King promise.

This is always the measure of a good offensive move. Ask yourself: Can the defender match it without undermining its own position?

A strength is also a weakness. But you must find the seam that holds the strength together.

Have it your way

"Have it your way" is fundamentally a good way to differentiate Burger King from McDonald's, but the negatives tend to outweigh the positives. The last thing a fast-food restaurant should do is to slow down its service, which customizing the burgers tends to do.

With all the line extensions that have taken place at McDonald's, it would be interesting to see what McDonald's might have become if it hadn't added all those items to its menus. Fortunately, there is a burger chain that has stayed true to the original McDonald's concept. It's In-N-Out Burger, located in California and a few other western states. In-N-Out Burger sells nothing but burgers, French fries, and drinks, but its average per-store sales ($1,976,990) are higher than McDonald's ($1,632,600).

McDonald's turns chicken

And fish and barbecue ribs and scrambled eggs. The seventies were the era of line extension at McDonald's as the chain looked for ways to bring in new customers and up the average check.

As desirable as these goals are, they are always dangerous. As you spread your line, you become vulnerable in the middle. Besides, if people wanted chicken, why wouldn't they go to a Kentucky Fried Chicken?

McDonald's first two major extensions, McChicken and McRib, were both failures.

Then came Chicken McNuggets, which were successful and which did add volume to McDonald's sales. But the new chicken product required a lot of effort and millions of advertising dollars.

What is surprising about Chicken McNuggets is Kentucky Fried Chicken's failure to respond. It took almost 8 years for the chicken chain to introduce their own version of McDonald's product. The name, of course, was simply Chicken Nuggets.

Defensive principle No. 3: *Strong competitive moves should always be blocked.* Kentucky Fried Chicken wasted 8 years. In those years they could have been using McDonald's advertising to drive business into the Colonel's place.

There's a difference in strategy between line extensions like the Egg McMuffin (the poor man's eggs Benedict) and Chicken McNuggets.

Breakfast is downtime at a burger place. Almost any breakfast item that brings in business would be a good strategy for a burger chain. A lunch or dinner item like McNuggets will take part of its volume from the chain's hamburger sales. Why spend millions to get a customer to order Chicken McNuggets instead of a Big Mac?

What wasn't thought out clearly at McDonald's and the other chains was the difference between the products they sold. Every marketer has three kinds of products: one kind of product to advertise, one kind to sell, and one kind to make money on.

It's wasteful to advertise a product just because you can sell it and make money on it, even if you can make big money on it.

Would a motion picture theater advertise the popcorn it sells? No, you advertise the movie and you make money on the popcorn and the drinks.

Automobile dealers advertise a car at its stripped price and hope they don't sell one that way because they make their real money on the automatic transmission, power brakes, AM/FM radio, and the other accessories.

Conceptually, a burger chain advertises the burger, sells the french fries along with the burger, and makes money on the soft drinks. That's the pattern that will drive profits down to the bottom line. If the kids drink enough of your 90-cent Cokes, you can almost afford to break even on everything else.

The biggest mistake companies make is confusing the product they sell with the products they should advertise. It doesn't matter so much what you sell to a customer once that customer is in the store. But advertising the same item might be a big mistake if it undermines your position.

McDonald's has broadened its menu so that today a McDonald's restaurant is "just another coffee shop," which sets up opportunities for competitors to attack the chain with a narrow approach.

Selling fish sandwiches is one thing; advertising fish sandwiches is another. Especially if the inclusion of that product undermines your hamburger position.

McDonald's started the game by attacking the coffee shop at Hamburger Hill in the middle of the line. It would be ironic if in the process of chasing business on the periphery, McDonald's turns itself into a chain of coffee shops that sell everything.

Me too, says Burger King

As the eighties rolled around, it was Burger King's turn to follow suit. As one Burger King executive said, "I never heard so much talk about a competitor. If McDonald's did something, we did it. If they didn't, we didn't."

Burger King kept introducing a variety of short-lived sandwiches, from veal parmesan to roast beef. Not to mention ham and cheese, deep-fried boned chicken breast, fish filet, and steak. "We lost sight of our identity," said that same executive.

Franchises weren't impressed. They kept reminding management that the company's name was Burger King, not Sandwich King.

The chain even copied Ronald McDonald with a character called the Magical Burger King in order to lure kids and their parents into the establishment.

By fiscal 1982 Burger King's sales had slowed down. That year they registered only an 8 percent increase in pretax earnings. By contrast, McDonald's aftertax net was up 15 percent.

Tampering with the product was one thing; tampering with the profits was another. Finally, the parent company sent in one of its Pillsbury dough boys to take charge. A few of the oddball sandwiches were knocked off the menu, but the biggest change came in advertising.

The battle of the burgers

Burger King turned again to the middle of McDonald's line. The classic offensive strategy of exploiting a weakness inherent in a leader who has overextended its line.

The most effective commercial was one that implied that Burger King hamburgers taste better because they are flame-broiled as compared with McDonald's hamburgers, which are fried.

"Broiling vs. frying," instantly captured the attention of the public and the lawyers at McDonald's who promptly filed suit.

It was the best thing that happened to Burger King. McDonald's indignant reaction catapulted the campaign into a story for all three television networks and dozens of TV stations and newspapers around the country.

Burger King's sales jumped, averaging 10 percent over the previous year as compared with a 3 percent gain for McDonald's. Small numbers, perhaps, but on a big base and on a battleground fought over with great intensity and enormous expenditures.

While Burger King couldn't match McDonald's advertising budget, they did manage to scrape together $120 million for their television effort.

Broiling not frying

"Broiling, not frying" is the best campaign that Burger King has ever run. The company should never have discontinued it. Furthermore, it should have reinforced the idea at the point of purchase. Instead of "Home of the Whopper," the sign out front should have said, "Home of the Broiled Burger."

Meanwhile, as Burger King was busy launching these offensive attacks, another chain was using a different marketing warfare strategy.

Flanking McDonald's

Founded by a former Kentucky Fried Chicken vice president, Wendy's didn't build its first Old Fashioned Hamburger stand until 1969.

After a late start, Wendy's came on fast with a flanking move at the adult end of the burger market. Stressing adult-size portions in a comfortable atmosphere, Wendy's makes its pitch to grownups. No free hats or balloons. Have it your way at Wendy's meant, "Without pickles, without relish, and without kids."

At Wendy's the smallest hamburger is a quarter-pounder which is shaped square so that it sticks out of the bun.

"Hot 'n juicy" was the advertising strategy that drove the adult burger idea into the public's consciousness. Wendy's hot 'n juicy hamburgers require "lots of napkins," the commercials tells us.

You wouldn't give your kids a burger like that. You'd have to change their clothes when you got them home.

Soon Wendy's profit margins were almost twice the average for fast-food restaurants, and it was pressing Burger King. (In fact, Wendy's unit profitability exceeded Burger King's.)

Then came that octogenarian wonder, Clara Peller. No single line in a television commercial has ever caught the imagination of the public as much as "Where's the beef?"

"Where's the beef?" helped boost Wendy's sales in 1984 by 26 percent. It was the first slogan in several years to become part of the vernacular, being mouthed by Walter Mondale and a host of others.

But more important in helping Wendy's sales was the fact that the slogan captured the essense of Wendy's strategy: the bigger burger for the adult-size appetite.

What came next is proof that strategy should dominate avertising, not vice versa. The same writer, the same art director, the same producer, and the same director teamed up to do "parts is parts." The line knocks competitors's chicken made of processed chicken parts. (Wendy's offers "100 percent natural boneless breast of chicken.")

Like McDonald's before it, Wendy's had chickened out. What happened? Nothing.

What Wendy's should do is to bring back the beef and bring back Clara Peller. In flanking, the pursuit is just as critical as the attack itself.

When Clara Peller died, Wendy's also laid to rest its "Where's the beef?" slogan. We think this was a mistake. A good position never dies. Witness the continuing success of "A diamond is forever" (57 years old), "Marlboro Country" (51 years old), and "The ultimate driving machine" (33 years old).

The low-end guerrilla

No burger war discussion would be complete without a mention of White Castle. Founded in 1921 and located in the northeast and upper midwest, the small 170-unit chain continues to do business exactly the way it has always done business.

"There's very little permanent in the world," said a customer, "but when I go to White Castle, I can have the same kind of hamburger I had when I was 5 . . . 35 years ago."

White Castle is still with us, demonstrating the strength of a smaller company that practices guerrilla tactics. Per-store sales are now $1,308,300 a year.

Devotees call the White Castle Hamburger a "slider" for reasons you wouldn't want to know about. A nostalgia burger is another way to look at the product's appeal.

Even more remarkable is the fact that each one of those Depression-era porcelain steel buildings does $1.28 million in volume a year, topping even McDonald's on a per-establishment basis.

Guerrilla principle No. 2: *No matter how successful you become, never act like the leader.* At White Castle, there are no Egg McMuffins, no Whoppers, no hot baked potatoes with choice of four different fillings, no Hamburger University.

There's more than one way to sell a hamburger, as long as you use appropriate strategy. So White Castles peacefully coexist with their big aggressive neighbors.

In such things as war, the errors which proceed from a spirit of benevolence are the worst.   Karl von Clausewitz

The computer war

The Coca-Cola of the computer war is IBM. And, so far at least, Big Blue is doing a better job of defending its position than Big Red.

IBM consistently hammers its competition into the ground. Students of marketing warfare have no reason to complain. There's no spirit of benevolence in Armonk.

"Live and let live" is not one of IBM's philosophies. It hasn't hesitated to crush its competition when the occasion demanded. Before you criticize IBM's conduct, you should understand the full nature of the computer war. At several key points in IBM's history, a failure to use force would have cost the company dearly.

The competitor you fail to crush in the morning will remain in the field to crush you in the afternoon.

Sperry Rand vs. IBM

In 1943 a teacher and a graduate student at the University of Pennsylvania built the first electronic digital computer.

Called ENIAC, an acronym for Electronic Numerical Integrator and Calculator, the 30-ton monster was a thousand times faster than any analog machine.

John W. Mauchly was the teacher, and J. Presper Echkert the student. After selling their company to Sperry Rand, the two devised other machines, among them the celebrated UNIVAC, developed in 1950.

In 1951 the Univac Division of Sperry Rand delivered the world's first commercially sold computer (to the U.S. Bureau of the Census).

A few years later IBM jumped into the market and the battle was joined. At stake: control of the most significant product development of the twentieth century.

This issue was decided in a skirmish between two relatively small companies in a short period of time. Each side had its strengths. Sperry Rand had the advantage of technological leadership. IBM had the advantage of an established position in the office market.

The battle could have gone either way. It was the early and strenuous effort, the application of the principle of force, that decided the issue.

Once IBM got on top, IBM stayed on top. Marketing battles are not like basketball games, with first one side ahead and then the other.

Marketing battles are more like military ones. Says Clausewitz: "The course of a battle resembles rather a slow disturbance of equilibrium than an oscillating to and fro, as those who are misled by mendacious descriptions usually suppose."

Most marketing people will never get the opportunity to participate in such an elementary struggle as the one

---

UNIVAC
vs.
IBM

We were wrong. It was Remington Rand's Univac, not Sperry Rand's Univac. Remington Rand merged with Sperry in 1955 to form Sperry Rand. In 1979, the name was changed to Sperry Corp. In 1986, Sperry merged with Burroughs to form Unisys. Multiple name changes like these tend to undermine the power of a brand, as well as confuse the authors of books.

between IBM and Sperry Rand in the fifties. But if you do, remember what Clausewitz says: "A general must strive to throw every weight into the scale in the first battle, hope and strive to win everything by it."

The need to establish your superiority early in the game is a key concern of a good marketing general. It's like the game of chess where the taking of a single pawn early in the game is usually enough to guarantee the victory.

After its victory over Sperry Rand, IBM consolidated its gains. Even though other companies jumped into the computer business, year after year IBM captured 60 to 70 percent of the market. People began calling the computer industry Snow White and the seven dwarfs.

The first all-out assault on Fortress IBM came in the early seventies from one of the dwarfs. But instead of a serious challenge it was a replay of Balaclava, 1854.

You can't win by emulating the leader. Companies get this wrong all the time. They try to find out how IBM does it, so they do the same thing. RCA even went out and hired ex-IBM executives to run their computer operation.

You can only win by turning the leader's strategy upside down. By finding the weak point in the leader's strength. By flanking. By becoming a guerrilla. By concentrating your forces.

After RCA and GE went under the Big Blue waves, it was now up to the five competitors that remained, collectively called the BUNCH (Burroughs, Univac, NCR, Control Data, and Honeywell). Who would be next to mount a threat to IBM? Actually, none of these.

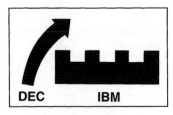

DEC (Digital Equipment Corporation) flanked IBM at the low end.

DEC vs. IBM: round 1

At the time the big companies were breaking their picks trying to get a piece of mainframe business away from IBM, a small start-up company was scoring a major computer marketing victory. It was Digital Equipment Corporation with a classic flanking attack.

IBM made big computers; DEC made small computers. IBM sold to the end-user; DEC sold to the OEM (original equipment manufacturer). IBM gave away the software; DEC pretended it didn't know what computer software was.

This was exactly the same flanking strategy used by Volkswagen and hundreds of other companies.

In 1965, DEC introduced the PDP-8, the first in a line of minicomputers, products that would become widely used in scientific research, education, industrial controls, and health care.

Then IBM made one of their rare mistakes. They failed to cover the DEC attack. Defensive principle No. 3: *Strong competitive moves should always be blocked.*

Leaders tend to be easier to flank at the low end. IBM's ego got in the way of its judgment. Who'd buy a low-cost, bare-bones, small computer without IBM software and IBM technological support?

Thousands of companies would and did. Sales of DEC minicomputers took off like a rocket. Digital Equipment became the darling of the stock market. In time DEC sales would soar past the $4 billion mark.

Hewlett-Packard, Data General, Honeywell, and others jumped on the minicomputer bandwagon. But not

IBM. It wasn't until 1976 that Big Blue entered the market with its Series 1 minicomputer.

But not even IBM can give away 11 years and expect to recoup. IBM never got more than a 10 percent share of the minicomputer market. DEC continues to dominate the market with a share in the neighborhood of 40 percent.

By the late seventies, the computer world had changed again. Young upstarts like Apple, Radio Shack, and Commodore introduced a new word into the vocabulary: the personal computer.

The stage was set for a replay of David vs. Goliath.

DEC went on to become the second-largest computer company in the world. You don't get to be No. 2 by emulating the leader. You get to be No. 2 by being the opposite of the leader. This is a general principle that is true of most markets.

DEC vs. IBM: round 2

Both DEC and IBM had watched from the sidelines as an entire industry developed from an 8-bit microprocessor or "computer on a chip."

Soon there were scores of companies making micro- or personal or home computers.

What were these little beasts? And what did one do with them? Did you use them in the home to play games? In school to learn computer science? At the office to do word processing or bookkeeping?

The answer turned out to be all these things and more. In truth, the microcomputer (or personal or home computer) was really a small general-purpose computer. For a few thousand dollars a personal computer could do many of the jobs that used to require a $1 million mainframe.

**World's largest maker
of small computers.**

Digital Equipment had a
powerful position that it should
have vigorously defended. It
was the world's largest maker
of small computers. We urged
Ken Olsen, president of DEC,
to be the first to launch a
serious, 16-bit business
computer. "Beat IBM to the
punch" was our advice. But
Olsen thought later was better.
"That way," he said, "we can
beat their specs." In the battle
between first and better, first
usually wins.

This was territory that belonged to DEC. In hindsight,
it's easy to say that DEC should have defended its small
computer position. But you don't have to be a prophet to
know the correct marketing moves if you have an understanding of strategy.

By the end of the seventies DEC was in an exceptionally strong position. And perhaps the lack of an early
counterattack by IBM made DEC a bit overconfident.

In military terms, DEC had completed its flanking
maneuver and should have shifted its strategy to defending its small computer territory. Defensive principle No.
2: *The best defensive strategy is the courage to attack yourself.*
DEC should have been one of the first to attack its minicomputer position with a microcomputer.

But DEC didn't have the courage or perhaps the foresight. Said DEC president Kenneth H. Olsen, "The personal computer will fall flat on its face in business."

It was perhaps the biggest misjudgment in American
business history since Henry Ford's failure to block General Motors' high-end flank.

Ken Olsen is a computer genius, but even a genius can
be wrong. As Fiorello LaGuardia once said, "I don't make
many mistakes, but when I make one, it's a beaut."

DEC could have been a computer giant, perhaps bigger than Big Blue, if they had moved into personal computers early and decisively. For there was one important
factor in the situation that most marketing people
overlooked.

The personal computer was being bought not as a personal computer, but as a business computer that was used
in the home or the office. And there were no personal

computer manufacturers with business credibility in the market. They all had home or hobby reputations.

Was General Motors going to equip its corporate offices with Radio Shack TRS-80s? (Known affectionately by the hobbyists as the Trash 80.) Or Commodore Pets or Apple IIs?

DEC fiddled while the lights were burning late in Boca Raton in preparation for the introduction of the IBM PC.

While DEC should have concentrated on protecting its small computer position, it fragmented its efforts in four separate uncoordinated areas.

1. DEC opened up a few dozen retail stores in competition with Radio Shack, ComputerLand, and thousands of independents. A weak offensive attack against dug-in competitors.

2. DEC took a flyer in word processors, going against a strong Wang and a host of specialists such as CPT, NBI, and Lanier.

3. DEC continued to push its minicomputer line higher and higher until they were in virtual competition with IBM's mainframes. This supermini battleground absorbed much of DEC's talent and resources.

4. DEC expended much effort and resources in developing elaborate office automation systems.

On the financial front, DEC put up $24 million to help finance Trilogy Ltd., a high-technology company started by Gene Amdahl to build a superfast computer to rival IBM's top-of-the-line mainframes.

Gateway to Lay off 2,500 With Closing of 188 Retail Stores

Headline from the April 2, 2004 issue of *The New York Times*. Gateway is just one of many computer manufacturers to open retail stores, only to close them a few years later. Strategically, several things go wrong when a manufacturer opens a retail chain. Not only does the company divide its forces by opening a second front, but it also competes with its customers, the retailers that handle its line. Yet the urge to expand distribution is exceptionally strong. Gateway is probably not the last company to learn that retail stores generally don't work for a manufacturer. We expect Apple Computer to learn this lesson after its red-hot iPod cools down.

On the one hand, DEC had all these ventures going on the periphery of its computer business. On the other hand, DEC refused to launch the one product that could protect its base of operations.

In 1980 DEC was the world's largest maker of small computers. In 1981 IBM launched the PC.

DEC vs. IBM: round 3

The instant success of the IBM PC didn't surprise the world. Conventional wisdom credits the power of those three initials—IBM—for doing the job. Which wasn't quite true.

Sure, IBM owned a powerful position in computers, but the position IBM occupied was in big computers. They had no credentials in small computers; that position was owned by DEC. But in the absence of Digital Equipment, IBM met no resistance in taking over the business side of the personal computer market. And then everyone noticed what should have been clear from the outset. The personal computer was much better suited to the business market than the home market.

Luck plays a far larger role in marketing than most experts will admit. And even the biggest companies like IBM get their share. In the 6 years that passed between the original Altair and the IBM PC, no serious business computer was introduced by a company with a reputation in the business market.

There were two small sorties in that direction, but they didn't amount to much. In January 1980 Hewlett-Packard introduced the HP-85, a lukewarm imitation of the Apple

The high point of IBM's domination of the personal computer market came in January 1983, when *Time* magazine named the PC its "Machine of the Year."

II, but they introduced the product as a scientific and professional machine, not a business one. And in July 1981 Xerox introduced the 820.

But Xerox was a copier company in the minds of the market. One hot summer month wasn't long enough to change that perception. And on August 12, 1981, IBM dropped its PC bombshell. And suddenly the game changed.

As the first business computer company to introduce a personal computer, IBM rapidly took over the battle. There was no one to defend the market because no one owned the position. Furthermore, there was an established market for personal computers because thousands of business people were already buying them from home computer companies like Apple and Radio Shack.

The opportunity for Digital Equipment and Hewlett-Packard vanished as IBM built up its momentum at the low end of the market.

Sixteen years earlier, DEC had successfully flanked IBM with the minicomputer. Now IBM, using the same strategy, had successfully flanked DEC with the personal computer.

DEC didn't respond to IBM's move until May 10, 1982, when the company introduced its own personal computer. And DEC made a fundamental error in the introduction.

DEC was now on offense and had to find a hole in IBM's line. Offensive principle No. 3: *Launch the attack on as narrow a front as possible.* Incredibly DEC introduced not one, but three personal computers: the Rainbow, the Professional, and the DECmate.

Defenders can sometimes profit by fielding a full line of products. It's almost always a mistake for an attacker to do so, as Digital Equipment found out.

The full line is a luxury to be enjoyed only by leaders. With no focus, a three-product strategy was doomed to failure. By 1984 IBM was outselling DEC more than 10 to 1 in personal computers. With inventory building up, DEC ceased production of the Rainbow (which turned out to be the biggest seller of the three) early in 1985.

Earlier in the game Ken Olsen was quoted as saying that DEC did not mind being last into a marketplace. The obvious implication was that the last one into the pool is able to adjust the product, its features, and its price in order to outperform the competition.

It's a reflection of the deeply held conviction among management people that in a marketing battle the better product usually wins.

Yet most computer experts agree that unlike the Altair and Apple that preceded it, the IBM PC brought no new technology to the market. IBM won the PC war with the same weapons available to everyone else.

It's a situation not unlike real warfare. Did the Allies win World War II because we had weaponry superior to the Germans'? Did we lose the Vietnam War because we had inferior weapons? The principle of force decided those military wars, and the principle of force decided the personal computer war.

But the computer industry was going to have to learn those lessons all over again.

The denouement of the DEC saga came a decade later when the company's founder was forced out. "Empire Ken Olsen built is crumbling," said *USA Today* in its July 17, 1992, issue. Is it possible that one strategic mistake (the failure to launch a personal computer early in the game) led to the ultimate destruction of a once-great company? We think so.

Everybody vs. IBM

Almost immediately the competition reacted by blasting away at IBM in an orgy of advertising recklessness.

"Dimension. The most powerful, most compatible personal computer you can buy," said one headline. "At about the same price as the IBM PC, it's obviously the best value you can find," said the copy of Dimension's ad.

"How to get an IBM PC for just $1995," said another competitor. "Buy a Chameleon," said the ad copy.

The personal computer war seemed to bring out the worst in corporate egos: macho posturing.

"You can't take on IBM and Wang on guts alone," said a Syntrex ad in an obvious attempt to prove their manhood. (No, Syntrex, you can't take on IBM and Wang on guts alone. You need money and you need a lot of it.)

"Why should you buy a business computer from a company you probably never heard of?" asked a three-page advertisement from TeleVideo. The ad introduces systems which "deliver more performance and reliability for the money than the companies you have heard of."

Not only the unknown but also the well-known companies jumped on IBM. "We're gunning for IBM," said Wang in a campaign that was typical of the times. "We're ready and eager to go head to head against IBM."

Even AT&T Information Systems took a shot. "At this stage of the personal computer game," said an AT&T ad, "you really ought to know the score." Speed, expandability, graphics, compatibility, and a category called "Etc." made up a computer scorecard. And the score? Five to nothing in favor of AT&T over IBM. (But the market voted 50 to 1 in favor of IBM over AT&T.)

Another well-known company that took a poke at IBM was Texas Instruments. "TI dares to compare," said the

Here is the Syntrex advertisement attacking IBM and Wang head-on. In addition to guts and money, you also need a lot of stupidity to do this.

A Wang advertisement attacking IBM.

For your child! The most marvelous, expensive, crazy (like a fox) Christmas gift of all time. A personal computer.

Radio Shack
The biggest name in little computers

Why would you call your personal computer brand "Radio Shack"? Furthermore, why would you give it a model name like "TRS-80," which just encouraged users to call it "Trash 80"? This kind of naming strategy could work only in a market with no competition. At one point in time, the TRS-80 was the largest-selling personal computer. ("The biggest name in little computers," is how the ad put it.) It's easy to see why the Radio Shack personal computer brand is no longer with us.

headline of an ad comparing its business computer with IBM's.

Unfortunately, Texas Instruments is well known for some of its failures. In 1983, for example, the company folded its home computer business and took a $660 million operating loss and write-down. (If you can't make it competing with Atari, Commodore, and Apple, how are you going to make it in the ring with King Kong?)

And Radio Shack ran a full-page ad in *The Wall Street Journal,* saying that its Tandy 2000 is "clearly superior to IBM, AT&T, Compaq, Apple, and Hewlett-Packard."

Every Manny, Moe, and Jack was claiming that their computers were better than IBM's. But a company called Leading Edge went one step further.

"The day the IBM Personal Computer became obsolete," was the modest headline of their ad. "It was a Monday in the autumn of '83," said the copy, "the day they announced the Leading Edge PC, a personal computer that's just plain better than the IBM PC, at just about half the price."

Now that your IBM PC was obsolete, the helpful folks at Monroe told you what to do with it. "Some respectful suggestions on other uses for yesterday's computer." The Monroe ad suggested using your IBM PC as a water cooler or maybe a desk lamp. "The new standard of microcomputers," said the ad, "is the Monroe System 2000."

In 1982 computer companies spent less than $1 billion on advertising. Two years later, they were up to more than $3 billion a year, outspending cars and cigarettes, to name two highly promoted product categories.

With this torrent of competitive attacks, did IBM strike back? Of course not. That's not good defensive strategy.

IBM vs. IBM

Once IBM had gotten a stranglehold on the PC market, they turned their guns around and used classic defensive strategy.

Attack yourself. It worked for Gillette, it worked for General Motors, and it worked for IBM.

Advance knowledge of this tactic actually helps IBM. Customers know Big Blue will constantly introduce new and better products that make IBM's own products obsolete.

"Cheaper and better than IBM," is actually IBM's strategy. It's hard for competitors to hit a target that's constantly moving. And customers and prospects have proved that they will wait for IBM's new products.

In relentless fashion they appeared on the personal computer battleground. The first was the PC XT, which had a hard disk drive which the owner could use to store up to 5000 pages of text.

Next was the PC AT, with a totally new microprocessor. "IBM's AT computer," reported *The Wall Street Journal,* "puts pressure on rivals and rest of its PC line. Surprisingly low-priced but remarkably powerful, the AT promises a broad appeal that is forcing IBM competitors to rethink their products and strategies," said the paper. "An industry consultant expects the PC AT to surpass the

IBM PC
IBM XT
IBM AT

"Attack yourself" is the strategy of a market leader, and that's exactly what IBM did with its PC line. After the August 1981 introduction of the PC, IBM followed with the XT model and then the AT model. Strangely enough, that seemed to be the end of the line. From then on, there were no PC introductions from IBM that had the impact of the XT and the AT, allowing Compaq to preempt the next generation of personal computers.

combined sales of the original Personal Computer and the PC XT model within a year."

The introduction of the AT model was met with silence from IBM's competitors. "IBM entry unchallenged at show," reported *The New York Times.* The show was Comdex, the industry's premier trade show, which draws 100,000 visitors. "Not a single major IBM competitor showed a machine to challenge the PC AT," said the *Times.*

No wonder a "solemn air pervades computer exhibition," as reported by the newspaper. "The personal computer industry appears to be trapped in a giant rut," said John Sculley of Apple.

A rut named IBM.

It wasn't long before the same publications that carried the advertising attacks on IBM began to report the casualties among the attackers. Raytheon dumped its Data Systems Division and took a $95 million after-tax loss. Computer Devices, Gavilan Computer, Osborne Computer, Victor Technologies, and Franklin Computer went Chapter 11.

Pitney Bowes dropped word processors and took a $22.5 million after-tax loss. Eagle Computer, Fortune Systems, Columbia Data Products, and Vector Graphic started to run up heavy losses.

Fear stalked Silicon Valley. And it wasn't helped when IBM started running ads exploiting the situation: "What most people want from a computer company is a good night's sleep."

To think of IBM as "all-powerful" is to make the opposite mistake. Companies, like armies, have power,

"A good night's sleep" is perhaps the most famous advertisement that IBM has ever run. The ad reinforced the perception in the marketplace that IBM might be more expensive, but it would always be there to protect its customers. (Nobody ever got fired for buying IBM.) This perception is one reason that IBM has done so superbly with its global services operation. Today, some 60 percent of IBM's business is software and services. Hardware is the smaller segment.

but only in the territory they occupy. IBM can be had. One mental territory that IBM does not own is in the home.

Apple vs. IBM: round 1

Apple polished off its competitors with the Apple II, the first "packaged" personal computer. Furthermore, its "open architecture" encouraged hundreds of companies to design software and hardware components to handle thousands of applications. Soon Apple had the largest piece of the personal computer pie. Then it protected its position using classic defensive strategies.

First came the II Plus. Then the IIe. Each machine was compatible with the previous design, each could use the same software, and each was designed to replace its predecessor. (The best defensive strategy is the courage to attack yourself.)

The Apple II was the first "packaged" personal computer. This was the product that built the brand and also built the perception that Apple was a "home" computer.

Then came the portable model, the IIc. Although not designed as a replacement for the IIe, it offered improved performance at a lower price; so in a sense it did compete with the IIe.

Apple had far less success with the Apple III, the only model not designed as a home computer. The Apple III was designed for an office environment and could not offer the same software as the II line which it was designed to complement rather than replace. The III had a lukewarm reception by the industry, an ominous sign of things to come.

It was against this backdrop that the all-powerful Armonk juggernaut launched the PCjr. "D Day for the

Bring an IBM PCjr home for the holidays.

IBM

IBM had a powerful position in the office, but it had no position at all in the home. Why would it have thought that an IBM home personal computer would be successful? And especially with a name like PCjr?

home computer," said *Time* magazine, who predicted big things ahead. "Marching from success to success," said the magazine, "IBM now has a product for the living room."

But the living room belongs to Apple.

In spite of a free keyboard retrofit, a one-third price cut, and $100 million worth of Charlie Chaplin, the PCjr failed to get off the ground.

Less than 18 months after D day, the PCjr was dead, killed by newly installed management at IBM's Entry Systems division.

The PCjr failure might have hurt IBM's ego but not its pocketbook. In its last full year, the PCjr accounted for only $150 million in revenues, peanuts compared with IBM's $46 billion in total revenues.

Doubters will say it wasn't the strategy, it was the product. Maybe, but there's too much evidence that a good product is not enough if you do not own the high ground. The victory usually goes to the side that controls the territory. This is the second principle of Clausewitz: the superiority of the defense.

The same thing happened to Big Blue when it tried to open retail stores in competition with ComputerLand, MicroAge, Entré, and others. "IBM's misadventures in the retail jungle," said *Fortune* magazine describing Big Blues problems.

Not only IBM but DEC, Xerox, and others have taken losses on the retail front. It's not your size that counts, it's your position. And none of the big manufacturers have retail strength in the prospect's mind.

Apple vs. IBM: round 2

The home is one thing. The office is another. The computer industry is now in the process of watching a rerun of Apple vs. IBM. Only this time the results are likely to be different because Apple is playing on IBM's territory. Apple is trying to move into the office vacuum left by the retreat of Digital Equipment Corp.

John Sculley and his Macintosh crew are spending $200 million a year in a major advertising campaign to try to take over the No. 2 position in office computers.

But Apple has a fatal weakness. Apple is a computer for the home, not the office.

Sculley is smart. You'll notice that his Macintosh ads almost never use the Apple name. He knows he has to position the Macintosh office apart from Apple's home position.

Unfortunately, the publicity continues to link Macintosh with Apple. This is the worm in Sculley's Macintosh.

Steve Wozniak, co-founder of Apple, resigned over the issue. "Apple's direction has been horrendously wrong for 5 years," he said.

The Woz also accused Apple's management of refusing to finance continued technical development of the Apple II personal computer.

We think Mr. Wozniak is right. Apple should concentrate on the home and small businesses.

CORPORATE PERFORMANCE

APPLE FINALLY INVADES THE OFFICE

As predicted, Macintosh never made much progress in the office market. According to *Fortune* magazine (Nov. 9, 1987), "A frontal assault three years ago flopped, so the company started pushing Macintoshes through corporate backdoors." That flopped, too, ultimately costing John Sculley his job. Today, Apple has just 3 percent of the worldwide market for personal computers.

In addition to the home and small business markets, another possibility for the Macintosh brand would have been graphics. If Apple had bought PowerPoint (which Microsoft did for $14 million), the combination of Macintosh and PowerPoint might have carved out a substantial share of the business market. In any case, the best strategy for an also-ran is to attack on a narrow front.

No. 2 vs. IBM

"The personal computer business today is much like the automobile industry in the early years of the twentieth

Compaq rose to the top of the personal computer field, at one point becoming the largest-selling PC brand in the world, with two brilliant flanking strategies. In March 1983, Compaq was the first company to introduce a "portable" computer; hence the name "Compaq." And in September 1986, Compaq was the first company to introduce a 16-MHz Intel 80386–based PC, the Compaq Deskpro 386. It was this latter move that propelled the company to the top of the field.

Incredibly, Dell Computer found a way to become the leader in personal computers—not by being better than the raft of competitors, but by being different. Dell was the first company to sell computers direct (first by phone and now by the Internet). This is a classic example of a flanking attack, perhaps the most powerful strategy in marketing. (In Dell's case, it was a distribution flank.)

century," said *Time* magazine. "Then, as now, a new technology was being developed with potentially revolutionary effects that attracted hordes of companies; some of them even had names like Apple and Commodore. Of course only a few of those early automakers survived."

"No one doubts IBM has become the General Motors of the personal computer industry. Now the question is who will become the Ford or Chrysler and who will be the Locomobile or Stanley Steamer?" concluded *Time*.

Who will become No. 2? As IBM continues to grow, it opens up a once-in-a-lifetime opportunity for a computer company to move in and become a strong No. 2.

Digital had the best chance. They were the world leader in small computers. They had a business name and a business reputation. But they threw it away.

Hertz and Avis. Coke and Pepsi. General Motors and Ford. McDonald's and Burger King. There's always room for No. 2.

There's a window of opportunity for someone else to move into the open position. There's no shortage of players either: AT&T, Burroughs, Compaq, Data General, Hewlett-Packard, ITT, Motorola, NCR, Sperry, Wang, Xerox, and Zenith.

And that list doesn't include the Japanese contestants: Epson, Fujitsu, Hitachi, Minolta, Mitsubishi, NEC, Oki, Panasonic, Sanyo, and Toshiba.

Confused? So is the potential customer. At this point in time, credentials are the most important selling tool. Customers are not buying a computer. They're buying a company. Look at the weaknesses of some of the players.

AT&T is a telephone company, not a computer company.

Burroughs is a mainframe company, and not a particularly strong one at that.

Compaq is a low-cost flanking move against IBM—very successful, but unlikely to be able to change its strategy to offensive warfare.

Data General is an also-ran to DEC in minicomputers.

ITT is a conglomerate. ITT isn't much of anything in the mind of the marketplace.

NCR means National Cash Register, not computers. Its major computer success has been in retail data entry systems where it can take advantage of its strength in cash registers.

Sperry is another also-ran in mainframes.

Wang is a maker of word processors. Wang has a chance, but their word processor position isn't helping them.

Xerox is a copier company. IBM couldn't make it in copiers. Xerox can't make it in computers.

Zenith makes television sets.

Forget the Japanese. Their deliberate, one-step-at-a-time approach can't cope with the fast-changing world of personal computers.

And guess who we think has the best opportunity? Hewlett-Packard.

That's right. We think Hewlett-Packard has the best opportunity to become the second largest computer company in the world. Hewlett-Packard is second only to DEC in minicomputers. Hewlett-Packard offers the same kind

We were wrong about the power of the IBM brand. In 23 years, the company reportedly lost about $15 billion on its PC line. We should have had the courage of our convictions that line extension is wrong. At the time, however, it was hard to be critical of a company that had 50 percent of the PC market.

We were right about the power of the Hewlett-Packard brand. Even though its strategy is a mess, H-P has the second-largest share of the personal computer market.

of user-friendly personal computers that Apple is pushing.

Hewlett-Packard can't do it by attacking IBM. Nobody can replace IBM.

Hewlett-Packard can do it by becoming the better business alternative to IBM than Apple. Then demonstrating to the marketplace that Hewlett-Packard means business.

The next few years will tell.

We fall into error if we attribute to strategy a power independent of tactical results.   Karl von Clausewitz

15 Strategy and tactics

The way to develop strategy, some companies believe, is to assemble three or four of their best people and lock them up in a room until they come up with the answer. "The ivory-tower think-tank approach," it is often called.

Other companies are fond of taking their entire senior management team to a conference center (or preferably a Caribbean island) to formulate plans for the future. The "get-away-from-the-phones, get-away-from-it-all" approach.

Both approaches attempt to get long-term strategic thinking as far away as possible from day-to-day tactical decisions. Both approaches are wrong.

One of the most important ideas derived from the study of warfare is the concept that tactics should drive strategy. First find a tactic that will work, and then build it into a strategy. Most companies do the opposite. They decide on the strategies they want to follow and then look around for the tactics that will make the strategies work.

Strategy follows tactics

As form should follow function, strategy should follow tactics. That is, the achievement of tactical results is the ultimate and only goal of a strategy. If a given strategy doesn't contribute to tactical results, then the given strategy is faulty, no matter how brilliantly conceived or eloquently presented. Strategy should be developed from the bottom up, not the top down.

Only a general with deep, intimate knowledge of what happens on the battlefield itself is in a position to develop an effective strategy.

Strategy should evolve out of the mud of the marketplace, not in the antiseptic environment of an ivory tower. (The armchair general out of touch with the battle has his counterpart in the conference-room CEO.)

The objective of a grand strategy is to make the operation work on a tactical level. It has no other purpose. In a military operation, the objective of the master plan, to put it bluntly, is to have two soldiers ready, willing, and able to fight at a place and moment in time where the enemy has only one. In other words, to facilitate the application of the principle of force on a tactical level.

A grand strategy may be awesome, inspirational, audacious, and bold, yet an utter failure if it doesn't put troops in the field in exactly the right place and at the right time to accomplish the job tactically.

There is no such thing as a bad strategy. Or a good one, for that matter. Strategies have no inherent merit in and of themselves. They are not like the plot of a novel or the outline of a movie, just waiting for someone to give them wings with the right words and music.

Unlike works of art which are often judged on their originality, creativity, and boldness of thought, marketing strategies should be judged for their effectiveness only at

Bottom-Up Marketing

By Al Ries & Jack Trout
Authors of *Positioning* and *Marketing Warfare*

The idea that tactics should drive strategy was the theme of our 1988 book, *Bottom-Up Marketing*. The book is still in print.

the point they come in contact with the customer and the competition.

In military warfare, the serious student of strategy begins with the study of the bayonet. It is no accident that perhaps the best military strategist the world has ever known began his career in the Prussian army at the ripe old age of 12.

Karl von Clausewitz knew what war was like because he had experienced it in all its horror. He was at Jena where he was captured by the French. He was at Borodino, the site of the massive confrontation between the armies of Napoleon and the armies of the Czar. He was at the Berezina River, one of the blackest sights in all history, where thousands of French were trampled under the horses of the Cossacks. He was at Waterloo.

His great strategic concepts were developed in the cauldron of practical experience. Clausewitz knew the importance of victory because he had tasted the bitterness of defeat so often in his career.

All the great military strategists have followed the same pattern. They learned strategy by first learning the tactics of warfare. Strategy follows tactics.

The strategic concepts of Karl von Clausewitz are so basic and so fundamental that they are still studied at West Point and at the other military academies of the world. Too bad that his masterpiece, *On War*, is not studied at Harvard and the other business schools of the world.

The artillery officer

In the late 1700s, no young man with royal blood or with royal connections would think of serving in the artillery. It was a noisy, dirty, backbreaking assignment. The MBAs of the day were in the cavalry, where the uniforms were terrific and you rode to work.

Napoleon was an ex-artillery officer who went on to become perhaps the world's greatest military strategist. Managers who become experts at handling the weapons of marketing have also gone on to have brilliant careers. Yesterday, the key weapon was television. Today, it's the Internet.

But war was changing at the tactical level. Except for reconnaissance, cavalry had almost ceased to play a role in the great land battles of the day. (No British square was ever broken by a cavalry attack.) The weapon that had assumed the key tactical role, the weapon that could cause the most casualties, was the artillery.

No one knew this better than Napoleon Bonaparte, the ex-artillery officer who became a general at the age of 24 and Emperor at 34.

The secret of Napoleon's strategic brilliance was his handling of artillery so that it would have the greatest effect at the tactical level. Napoleon consistently exploited the mobility of his artillery, massing his guns and sending them at the closest possible range to blast a gap for the infantry and cavalry.

"Artillery," said Napoleon, "holds the key to the true destiny of armies and nations. One can never have enough cannon."

The tank commander

Take an artillery piece, mount it on top of an internal combustion engine, add armor and tractor tracks, and what do you have? The tank, the twentieth century equivalent of the 6-pounders of Napoleon's day.

It's probably no accident that the best military strategist of World War II also learned his trade from the bottom up. George S. Patton, Jr., was an observer at Cambrai in 1917, when the English launched the world's first large-scale tank attack.

In 1918 Patton was appointed the first United States commander of armor. Later that year he led his tanks into battle in the Saint Mihiel salient.

Patton applied his knowledge of tank tactics in the Normandy breakout and in his wild, free-swinging 1944 dash through France where his Third Army broke every known record for taking ground.

For all of his excesses of character, Patton was an astute strategist whose military successes were based on sound concepts in the Clausewitz mold.

"One does not plan and then try to make the circumstances fit those plans," Patton said. "One tries to make plans fit the circumstances. I think the difference between success and failure in high command depends on the ability, or the lack of it, to do just that."

It was Patton's knowledge and use of armor, the key tactical weapon of World War II, that made him such a great military strategist. How many management people think of themselves as marketing strategists without knowing much about PR, television, the Internet, and the other weapons of a marketing program? Far too many.

The advertising expert

The tanks and artillery of today's marketing war is advertising. Until you know how to use advertising at the tactical level, you are at a severe disadvantage as a marketing strategist.

Because many management people are ignorant of the tactical applications of advertising power, they order the same kind of suicidal assaults against dug-in competition that took place in the trench warfare of World War I. "The enemy's rear is the happy hunting ground for armor," said Patton. "Use every means to get it there."

Apple didn't hire John Sculley because he knew how to run a bottling plant or the secret formula for Pepsi-Cola. Apple hired Sculley for his handling of advertising.

While the odds are against his Apple-in-the-office strategy (as they were against the old master at Waterloo), Sculley's advertising so far has been skillfully directed. His "1984" commercial with its George Orwell theme created more impact than any other single television message.

By no means are personal selling and the other weapons of marketing obsolete. Each arm has a vital role to play in a marketing war. (Just as the infantry did in Napoleon's day.) But advertising is the critical weapon which must be handled superbly if a company is going to win a big marketing victory.

(By advertising, of course, we mean all the mechanized forms of reaching the marketplace, including print and broadcast advertising, publicity, direct mail, sampling, sales brochures, displays. In the same sense, an armored corps includes self-propelled guns, armored personnel carriers, and an array of vehicles, including tanks.)

Critics could cite many examples where poorly handled advertising seemed to have no adverse effect. IBM's successful PC launch didn't seem to suffer from the use of Charlie Chaplin in IBM's advertising. True enough. Poor advertising is a minor hindrance for a powerful IBM. But poor advertising could be fatal for a company without IBM's depth of resources.

Strategy tolerates run-of-the-mill tactics

While strategy evolves from an intimate understanding of tactics, the paradox is that good strategy doesn't depend on superlative tactics. The essence of a sound strategy is to be able to win the marketing war without tactical brilliance.

IBM didn't need good advertising to win the PC war. IBM's strategy of being the first business computer company to introduce a personal computer assured the company of success before the product was launched. It was this strategy that made the tactics work beautifully. It was an understanding of tactics that convinced IBM to adopt this strategy.

While acknowledging the importance of the advertising arm, many corporate executives falsely rely it. They look for advertising to create the "master stroke" that will allow them to win the war. The Battle of the Bulge, Hitler's counterattack through the Ardennes in the winter of 1944, happens frequently in the marketing arena. Companies stake everything on a massive advertising program that will "save the situation."

These situations rarely get saved. The reasons are quite straightforward. If the strategy is good, the battle can be won with indifferent tactics. If superb tactics are needed to win the battle, then the strategy is not sound.

In other words, the company that relies on tactical brilliance is also relying on an unsound strategy. So now the company is going to war with two different ways to fail: (1) a poor strategy and (2) a dependence on tactical brilliance, which history shows happens infrequently.

The free world applauded when Patton raced across France. But the truth is, we would have won without him.

Nothing is absolute. In marketing as well as in military war, there are times when the odds are strongly against. "The more helpless the situation," says Clausewitz, "the

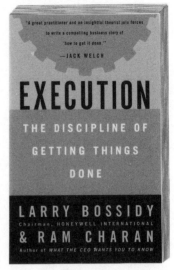

Many management books promote the idea that good execution will win any battle. A typical example is *Execution: The Discipline of Getting Things Done* by Larry Bossidy and Ram Charan.

more everything presses toward one single, desperate blow.''

In football, the long bomb is the desperation play, the one to call when everything else has failed. Most of the time, the grind-it-out tactics of a Procter & Gamble will win the day.

The marketing general that depends on superior tactics to win the war is usually quick to blame the arm that didn't work. And in today's battleground, that arm is usually the advertising.

Strategy directs tactics

The general that neglects the study of the tactical situation in the development of strategy often turns around and becomes too sensitive to tactics once the battle is launched.

If a strategy is soundly conceived from a tactical point of view, then the strategy ought to direct the tactics once the battle is started.

A good general has the ability to overlook tactical difficulties in order to press ahead to achieve the strategic objectives. At times it may be necessary to expend considerable resources in order to take key points that might be holding up the development of the overall strategy. You might, for example, have to operate a given business at a loss for a short period of time in order to achieve tactical objectives that allow a general strategy to succeed.

The reverse is also true. You might have to let business decline or eliminate profitable products if they are not consistent with your strategy. This can cause problems with a sales-oriented staff out for volume, whatever the consequences. Clausewitz consistently stresses the unity of strategy.

Clausewitz is quick to dismiss the idea that the taking of a certain geographic point or the occupation of an undefended province means anything unless it contributes to the operation as a whole. "Just as in commerce the merchant cannot set apart and place in security gains from one single transaction by itself," says Clausewitz, "so in war a single advantage cannot be separated from the result of the whole."

Twentieth century merchants like Coca-Cola sometimes forget a principle that nineteenth century merchants seem to have understood. They will introduce an easy product to sell like Diet Coke and then express surprise when their Tab business falls apart. To repeat: "A single advantage cannot be separated from the result of the whole."

A decentralized approach to management is the most common reason for the lack of strategic direction of a company's tactics. Like line extension itself, in the short term decentralized management can produce results. But in the long term, the company is bound to suffer. A case in point is ITT, which is currently paying the price for years of decentralized management.

Getting decision making out in the field is the rationale most decentralized organizations use to justify their existence. Getting out in the field to study the tactical situation is an essential part of developing a good strategy. But it's only one part. Someone still needs to tie the elements together into an organized coherent strategy.

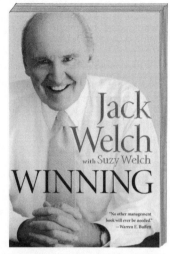

Even Jack Welch ("Manager of the Century," according to *Fortune* magazine) downplays the importance of strategy. "In real life," writes Welch in his latest book, *Winning*, "strategy is actually very straightforward. You pick a general direction and implement like hell." That might work for General Electric, which has a powerful leadership position in virtually all of its markets, but not for most companies.

Single point of attack

> "There's nobody in the world who doesn't believe that MCI can't pick off 15% of any market."
>
> "We could pick off that much of the shoe market, and we don't even make shoes."
>
> Bert Roberts, CEO.

Just because a company is successful in one market doesn't necessarily mean that it can be successful in another. Yet there are many managers who will gleefully attack any and all targets with a heavy dose of overconfidence. Witness what the former CEO of MCI has to say about the shoe market.

You knew that Exxon Office Systems was in trouble when the company ran an advertisement announcing its "commitment to the future." Only companies in trouble run ads saying that they're going to be around for the long run.

At any given point in time, one objective should dominate a company's strategic plans.

That one objective should have first call on the company's resources. You might call this concept a "single point of attack."

Decentralized management and a lack of a unified corporate strategy results in multiple points of attack, common in American business today. Some are successes, some are failures, and none are coordinated to build the business for the long haul.

Take Exxon's ill-fated venture into office products and systems: Qwip, Qwyx, Zilog, Vydec, Daystar, Dialog, and Delphi. These were some of the names Exxon used in its attack on the office market. But where was Exxon's corporate strategy? Oil and water mix a lot better than oil and office machines.

Contrast Exxon's fling with IBM's launch of the PC. There was an important strategic goal to be achieved with the PC: The company wanted to protect its mainframe business from being flanked at the low end. And IBM put a large share of its energies and a big chunk of its resources into the PC effort. (The same kind of thinking that resulted in the IBM 360/370 mainframe line a few decades earlier.)

Companies often equip divisions with money and material and then turn them out in the field with little or no direction. "Here, take these assets and make money with them," is a common direction for the company with multiple lines of attack.

As the company's divisions move out into the business world, they tend to limit their attacks to "targets of opportunity." There may be valid reasons why a given target is easy to take. The product may have no long-term future, for example.

Take word processors. As IBM moved more heavily into general-purpose office computers, it left the word processor market relatively open. So Lanier, CPT, NBI, and others jumped in to seize this target of opportunity. Where will these companies be tomorrow?

Did Warner Communications have a long-term corporate strategy when they bought Atari? Or were they just playing games?

Did General Mills have a strategic plan before they lost their shirt on Izod?

And what do you suppose Mobil had in mind for Montgomery Ward?

In the past, these corporate moves were justified by a fad called diversification. They all fly in the face of the most basic of all military maxims, the concentration of force.

Why would MCI, locked in battle with AT&T, one of the giant corporations of this world, open up a second front by launching MCI Mail? From a military point of view, this makes no sense at all. And as the losses at MCI Mail mount up, the move seems to make no marketing sense either.

What was General Motors trying to do when they drove down to Dallas and gave Ross Perot $2.5 billion for his Electronic Data Systems? Nothing strategic, you can be sure.

The late Roberto Goizueta, former head of Coca-Cola, once said: "There's a perception in this country that you're better off if you're in two lousy businesses than if you're in one good one—that you're spreading your risk. It's crazy."

Sony, of course, did not meet its goal of being a 50-50 company. If anything, Sony has more of a consumer focus today than it did 20 years ago.

It's bad enough when such moves are accidental. (They made us an offer we couldn't refuse.) It's worse when companies go out of their way to develop a diversification strategy.

Take Sony. According to *Fortune* magazine, Sony has developed a 50-50 strategy. By 1990 the company wants to be a half-consumer, half-nonconsumer company instead of the 80-20 company it is today. Does that make sense?

No. That's shifting resources from the battle you're winning to the battle you're losing. Furthermore, Sony is doing it at the very time they're facing a crisis on the consumer side of their business; what to do about the Betamax technology that has been steadily losing ground to VHS technology.

Attack and counterattack

To every action, states a law of physics, there is an equal and opposite reaction. Many marketing commanders draw up battle plans as if the enemy will make no response. Nothing is further from the truth.

The likelihood is just the opposite. Cut your price in half and your competitor is likely to do the same. To every action there is some reaction on the part of your competition, even if it doesn't exactly duplicate your initial move.

Don't get blind-sided. A good marketing strategy is one that anticipates the competitor's counterattack. Many of the principles of marketing warfare recognize the danger of counterattack. Offensive principle No. 2: *Find a weakness inherent in the leader's strength and attack at that point.* For leaders to block this kind of move, leaders would have to weaken their own strength, something they are going to be hesitant to do.

Another way to analyze the possibility of strong counterattacks is to look at predicted share of market changes. Some companies boldly predict they will take half of a leader's share, for example. Yet they fail to predict the clawing and scratching that will take place in the process. The wounded eagle response.

Expect the counterattack. Your competitors will spend far more money and make more sacrifices to protect what they already own than they would in an offensive attack on your position.

Apple's attack on the corporate market, of course, was a miserable failure. You can't go head-to-head against a superior enemy . . . in warfare as well as in marketing.

Action is not independent of strategy

Whatever action a company takes or intends to take cannot be divorced from the strategy that the action implies. The action is the strategy.

Yet many marketing people think they can separate the two. Apple, for example, has announced that it's going to invade the Fortune 500. Apple can't then sit back and say, "Now, what's our strategy going to be?" Invading the Fortune 500 is Apple strategy. Whether the invasion succeeds or not will depend primarily on whether the strategy yields tactics appropriate for Apple, considering the strength of the defender IBM.

Certainly Apple can increase its chances for success by following the principles of marketing warfare—launching the attack on a narrow front, for example. But these factors can only help to a degree. The more fundamental strategic question is: Can a small company with the resources of an Apple take on IBM on its home grounds?

Big successful companies get into trouble with the false notion that anything is possible if only the company has the will to succeed. They often decide what they want to accomplish and then assign a task force to develop the strategy to achieve their goals. No company is big enough to do this. Invariably there are objectives that are beyond their means.

Good marketing strategists live in the world of tactics and reality. They never let their egos get in the way of their judgment. They never attempt the impossible, nor do they push a campaign or line of attack beyond a reasonable goal. They focus their minds on what can be accomplished with the tactical tools available, not on grandiose schemes or impossible dreams.

Strategy cannot be divorced from tactics

If action implies strategy, then strategy implies tactics. There is a seamless quality about this continuum that will suffer greatly if you try to cut it at any point. A knowledge of tactics helps you develop the strategy which makes possible a certain course of action for the corporation.

Once this action is agreed to, the strategy takes over to direct the tactics. A rigid barrier between tactics and strategy would serve to frustrate the entire process.

Take advertising, the key component of most marketing wars. Companies normally hire agencies to handle the tactics of an advertising campaign. But the company normally develops the marketing strategy before the agency starts to work. In other words, the company decides what to do; the agency decides how to do it.

This sounds so simple and logical that it might seem impertinent to point out the fatal flaw in this arrangement. The artificial barrier between the two prevents the agency's specialized knowledge of tactics from being a major factor in the development of the company's strategy.

Does Miller Brewing appreciate the tactical difficulties of trying to establish two major brands under one brand name? Apparently not. Miller developed the strategy and then assigned the tactical jobs to their two advertising agencies. Did J. Walter Thompson question the strategy of trying to establish two major beer brands with the same name? Would you question a strategy that resulted in your getting a $50 million account? An account that generates $7.5 million in income for the agency every year?

To be truly effective in the marketing wars of tomorrow, advertising agencies will have to do more strategic planning or companies will have to learn more about advertising tactics. Both trends seem to be occurring at the same time.

At the moment, however, few agencies know how to turn their tactical knowledge of advertising into strategic programs, and few companies have a deep knowledge of advertising tactics.

Some agencies will strongly resist the demands for more strategic thinking, because if the truth were known, they just don't want to be held responsible for the success of advertising programs. They would rather blame the product or the sales force.

The use of reserves

No military commander would launch an attack without adequate reserves. "The number of fresh reserves," says Clausewitz, "is always the chief point looked at by both commanders."

The commander who has the larger reserve force is in the dominant position. Nor is it always necessary, or even desirable, to commit all your reserves to every battle.

No company would spend its entire annual advertising budget on January 1. Nor would a military general put every available soldier into the front line the moment his army collides with the other side. The use and handling of reserves is always a key issue in any battle.

A good general will try to win the victory without using all the reserves. Almost without exception, it's the losing army that has exhausted all its reserves.

What we're writing about, of course, are tactical reserves—forces that can be committed to a battle on a moment's notice. Strategic reserves are another matter. Armies cannot depend on soldiers that first have to be drafted and then trained. Clausewitz warns against relying on strategic reserves, which he considers a local inconsistency. If they are strategic, they are not reserves. That is, they are not immediately available to be thrown into the battle at the discretion of the field commander.

The entrepreneur who launches two businesses instead of one falls into the strategic reserve trap. One cannot be a reserve for the other since neither investment can be liquidated quickly in an emergency. Better to launch one business with liquid resources in reserve.

The same principle applies to those companies who attempt too much on too many fronts in too short a period of time. "Where are the reserves?" is the key question to ask.

Out of a thousand men who are remarkable, some for mind, others for boldness or strength of will, perhaps not one will combine in himself all those qualities which are required to raise a man above mediocrity in the career of a general.   Karl von Clausewitz

16 The marketing general

With few exceptions, colorless captains of industry maneuver their corporations on the marketing battlefields of the world without attracting much attention. Or for that matter without doing much to motivate or inspire their troops. (Some exceptions are Jack Welch of General Electric, Lee Iacocca of Chrysler, and John Reed of Citibank.)

Many corporate chieftains hide behind the two philosophy twins—diversification and decentralization—to keep themselves out of the limelight.

Business today cries out for more field marshals—more men and women willing to accept responsibility for planning and directing a total marketing program. At a time when business desperately needs big thinkers, business is going in the opposite direction. Diversification and decentralization are pushing strategy down the ladder. One Fortune 500 company bragged that half its managers are involved in strategic planning.

Patton's Third Army had 105 generals and one strategic planner.

The more people involved in the strategic process, the less likely the company is to come up with a brilliant strategy. We need to push the process up the ladder, not down.

Decentralization has dulled the risk-taking spirit of business people. Managers are not dummies. They know that if they can somehow get above the "firing line," they can coast to the top of their corporation.

It's easy to tell whether you're above or below the line in your company. You're below the line if you can be fired for not achieving your marketing objectives. You're above the line if you have someone you can fire for not achieving their objectives.

Note: When you're above the line, you personally don't have any marketing objectives. Naturally, you take credit for the successes in your area and you find someone to blame for the failures. You have achieved tenure in your corporation, a nice position to be in.

As decentralization has pushed the firing line lower and lower, companies have wound up with a collection of fiefdoms, none of which are powerful enough to launch a big marketing program on their own. So marketing at many companies has degenerated into a collection of small holding operations, what you might call trench warfare of the business world.

We believe that business is changing, that CEOs are starting to consolidate units so that they're big and powerful enough to launch effective marketing programs. As this happens, business faces another problem. Where are we going to find the marketing generals to run these expanded operations?

They're hard to find. Clausewitz noted that many otherwise intelligent people don't necessarily have the qualities to make a good general. Out of a thousand, perhaps one does.

What qualities does a marketing general need? Is there anything to learn from places like Virginia Military Institute, Annapolis, and West Point?

A marketing general must be flexible

The key characteristic of a marketing general is flexibility. It's not glamorous and it's not always recognized as a virtue, but no military general has been a big success without it. A general must be flexible enough to adjust the strategy to the situation and not vice versa.

Most would-be marketing generals do just the opposite. They start with a strategy that has worked in the past and then they analyze the situation. All too often they make the situation fit the strategy. It's not hard to do, because the "facts" are never clearcut.

Says Clausewitz: "A great part of the information obtained in war is contradictory, a still greater part is false, and by far the greatest part is of a doubtful character."

In the fog of war, it's all too easy to apply the tried-and-true strategy that worked in the past. Any other approach would seem the height of recklessness to a Johnny One-Note, who usually adds, "Let's go with what we know will work."

Flexibility.

Jack Welch of General Electric best demonstrates the flexibility required of a marketing general. He wasn't committed to any product or service. If it wasn't No. 1 or No. 2, he would fix it, sell it, or shut it down.

Sometimes this attitude is mistaken for strength. "He has the courage of his convictions" is a typical remark. A stubborn, inflexible attitude is a sign of weakness in a general, not strength.

Much meaningless posturing goes on in marketing today. A competitor cuts a price and management says, "They know what their product is worth."

An employee suggests attacking a competitor and management says, "We believe in the positive approach, in selling our products on their merits, not in denigrating our competitors' products."

A good general has no built-in biases. He or she will seriously consider all alternatives and listen to all points of view before making a decision.

It's this flexibility of mind that can terrorize the enemy's camp. They never know when or where the blow will strike. It's awfully hard to defend against what you're unprepared for.

A marketing general must have mental courage

No issue is as much discussed as the question of courage. A marketing general certainly needs courage.

What separates the good generals from the mediocre is the type of courage. A good general has an unlimited supply of mental courage to stand up to superiors and associates who may advocate a different approach. While a good marketing general has an openness of mind to listen to all points of view, at some point in time a decision must be made. This is when the open mind closes and the good general reaches deep inside to find the strength of will and mental courage to prevail.

Lee Iacocca puts it this way:

> If I had to sum up in one word the qualities that make a good manager, I'd say that it all comes down to decisiveness. You can use the fanciest computers in the world and you can gather all the charts and numbers, but in the end you have to bring all your information together, set up a timetable, and *act*.

Courage.

Lee Iacocca of Chrysler best demonstrates the courage required of a marketing general. He took over a company that was on the verge of bankruptcy and by a series of brilliant flanking moves turned Chrysler into a winner.

Mediocre generals are often macho types: "Nobody can tell me what to do." They are drawn to marketing because of its obvious parallels to military warfare. Often, too, they pick up the language of the military with much talk of troops and breakthroughs.

Macho types are quick to defend decisions made in the past. They seem to have an emotional commitment to past decisions and strategies. By their nature, macho types are drawn to the lost cause. The ultimate act of courage, it seems to them, is to die for your company.

The macho type may be a good leader, however. Leaders are not necessarily good generals or strategists. A vain, ego-driven person might be the perfect figurehead for a company that needs leadership more than strategy, a company where morale has fallen so low that an externally directed strategy has no hope of success. What such a company needs first is an internally inspired leader.

If you're good at acting, you can be a good leader as well as a good strategist. Patton used to practice his "war face" in front of a mirror. And Lee Iacocca fired up his troops with these immortal lines: "We have one and only one ambition. To be the best. What else is there?"

Meanwhile, back at the plant Iacocca's strategy was totally different.

The morale factor is overstressed by many consultants who believe that morale alone can create marketing victories. Not true, although the opposite is. There's nothing like a marketing victory to improve the morale of the troops.

Boldness.

Jeffrey Campbell of Burger King best demonstrates the boldness required of a marketing general. He launched a very successful attack against market leader McDonald's with his "broiling not frying" strategy.

A marketing general must be bold

Over the years, the military has praised physical courage and bravery, handing out millions of medals in the process.

As important as physical courage is to a fighting force, it's not a key attribute for the commander. A general is not a soldier. Too many generals have tried to act the part and have paid for their recklessness in defeat or excessive casualties.

In place of physical courage, marketing generals need boldness. When the time is right, they must be able to strike quickly and decisively. Too often, however, as they move up the ladder of success, marketing generals lose their spirit of boldness.

"Boldness becomes rarer, the higher the rank," says Clausewitz. Or the nearer to retirement. Or the greater the number of shares in the stock option plan.

Boldness is an especially valuable trait when the tide is running with you. That's when the marketing operation really can benefit from having a commander who knows how to pour it on.

Many marketing generals have a basic flaw in their nature. They exhibit too much courage when the deck is stacked against them. And too much caution when the cards are on their side.

A marketing general must know the facts

Generals generalize. So the feeling goes, you don't really have to know any of the details in order to work up a master strategy. As a matter of fact, the specialist is often treated with some disdain at the top echelons of management. Anyone who knows too much about any one field is not to be trusted to have a broad outlook.

Marketing strategy is easy. Anybody can do it. Every trade magazine editor seems to feel the urge to tell the corporations of America how to run their business.

Nothing could be further from the truth. To every marketing problem there is an easy and obvious answer, which is usually wrong. When Coca-Cola announced it was changing its formula, Coke's chairman bragged, "It's the surest decision we ever made." Also wrong.

"Everything is very simple in war," says Clausewitz, "but the simplest thing is difficult."

A good marketing general builds strategy from the ground up, starting with the details. When the strategy is developed, it will be simple, but it won't necessarily be the obvious answer.

Knowledge.

John Reed of Citibank best demonstrates the knowledge required of a marketing general. He pioneered Citibank's launch of ATM machines, which has revolutionized consumer banking.

A marketing general needs to be lucky

Luck plays a large role in the outcome of a marketing battle. After the planning, after the attack, you have to be

Luck.

Donald Trump is a charter member of the Lucky Sperm club. To his credit, The Donald has spent his career building up the family's fortune instead of spending his inheritance.

prepared for the luck of the draw. Sure, if you've done your job right, you have the odds on your side.

"No other human activity," says Clausewitz, "is so continuously or universally bound up with chance. War most closely resembles a game of cards."

When your luck runs out, you ought to be prepared to cut your losses quickly. "Capitulation is not a disgrace," says Clausewitz. "A general can no more entertain the idea of fighting to the last man than a good chess player would play an obviously lost game."

If Eisenhower could throw in the towel in Korea, a good marketing general ought to be able to know when it's time to quit. No purpose is served by wasting resources to conserve egos. Better to admit defeat and move on to another marketing war.

There are many more battles to fight and many more victories to win.

A marketing general should know the rules

To play any game well, you first have to learn the rules, or principles, of the game. And second, you have to forget about them. That is, you have to learn to play without thinking about the rules.

This is true whether the game is chess or golf or marketing warfare. Shortcuts won't work. You have to start by learning the rules and then practice enough to forget them.

A good tennis player doesn't think about how to hold the racquet or the finer points of stroke-making while playing the game. A tennis player concentrates on out-playing the opponent.

A would-be marketing general ought to learn the principles of marketing warfare first and then forget about them while playing the game. A good general shouldn't consciously ask: "What type of warfare are we fighting? And which principles should we be using?"

Good generals should know the rules so well that they can forget about them and concentrate on the opponents. Like good habits, rules are learned to be forgotten.

The problem with marketing today is not just the lack of rules. The biggest problem of all is the failure to realize that one ought to have rules in the first place.

To rectify that problem, marketing people must start to systematically examine the history of marketing and formulate the strategic principles that govern the outcome of corporate battles. Nothing today is as important as strategy.

Strategy and timing are the Himalayas of marketing. Everything else is the Catskills.

In today's corporate boardrooms, there are many Carly Fiorinas—great leaders, but poor strategists. For Hewlett-Packard to merge with Compaq Computer made no sense at all, except to investment bankers and self-important leaders.

Index

Epilogue

When we wrote this book 20 years ago, we never imagined that so many of America's big brands would end up in so much trouble. Icons like AT&T. General Motors, Kodak, and the like are supposed to be built to last.

Why, with all their armies, have they fared so poorly? Of course, you can say that they pursued bad strategy. But why? Many of the big brands that are in trouble were surrounded by consultants who took their money but apparently offered them no real help against the enemies that were threatening to overwhelm them.

One would think that the last line of defense against bad decisions would be the board of directors. Here you have a dozen or so wise people with decades of experience ready to keep the CEO and his or her senior officers on the straight and narrow. Right?

Wrong. It appears that too many directors are on too many boards and have little time to deal with problems that demand their full attention. Or they are friends of top management, not critics or advisors.

But if consultants and boards are of little help, at least they don't do too much damage. Occasionally, they even produce some good thinking. But to us, the biggest culprit is Wall Street. It is nothing but trouble, as it often creates an environment that encourages bad, sometimes irrevocable things to happen. In a way, it sets up a greenhouse for trouble, and, like a greenhouse, what it's all about is encouraging things to "grow."

The well-known economist Milton Friedman put it perfectly when he said, "We don't have a desperate need to grow. We have a desperate desire to grow." That desire for growth is at the heart of what can go wrong for many companies. Growth is the byproduct of doing things right. But in itself, it is not a worthy goal. In fact, growth is the culprit behind impossible goals and bad decisions.

In marketing warfare, it's not what you want to do, it's what the enemy (your competition) will let you do. It's not about the price of your stock. It's about how many customers you are winning versus your competitors.

Al Ries   Jack Trout